Fantastic Secrets Behind

Behind

Fantastic Beasts

S. P. Sipal

Deep River Press, Inc.
Sanford, North Carolina

Fantastic Secrets Behind Fantastic Beasts
ISBN 978-1945561061
Library of Congress Control Number 2016962390

Published by Deep River Press, Inc. December 2016

ILLUSTRATIONS by Kayla Laine Perkinson
COVER DESIGN by Greg Schultz

Contents

Dedication

To Bill Perkinson,
brother and friend,
without whose care and devotion to our father,
I could never have written this book.

Introduction

(The Game is Afoot)

Lumos. The magic begins.

No one knows how to string readers along from one clue to the next, one story to the next, quite the way JK Rowling does. The world-wide phenomenon that was Harry Potter kept fans scouring her text between releases to find the bits of detail they missed the first seven reads through. With these nuggets, from the young Colin Creeveys to the older Bathilda Bagshots, they would research arcane myths and esoteric knowledge to formulate their own theories. Then, they would plaster the Internet with speculation before the next book's release.

Those Harry Potter book releases were magical events. After acquiring their portkey into magic at midnight, readers stayed up eagerly to immerse themselves in a magical world that was home. Many were eager to see if one of their pet theories had been validated by the Headmistress herself.

Now the game is afoot again. Fans of the first generation and the new have gathered to savor the euphoria of the first film which expands the wizarding world in a time before Harry. Online and in person, fandom draws together to help each other penetrate the fog from Rowling's sleight of hand that obscures the hidden clues.

Jewels of questions beg us to consider:

- Is there an Animagi hidden in the story?
- Why will there be five movies?
- What secret is Modesty hiding?
- Did Frank wipe out all the memories from that fateful night?
- And was Grindelwald already in possession of the Elder Wand?

And treasures of clues entice us deeper:

- A possible new spell, more powerful than Avada Kedavra, that shoots in white light.
- A certain floor mosaic in an office at MACUSA that may spell the secret to the whole series.
- A tiny pigeon hiding in the rafters of the church.
- And the possibility of certain photographic evidence.

Join me on this grand adventure as we burrow beneath the surface of Rowling's texts in search of the treasure she's left for our discovery. Before that pilfering pest of a Niffler beats us to it!

About Me

I am a writer and editor who participated in the original Potter mania, including speaking at a fan conference in London the night of the Deathly Hallows' release. What an experience! As a fan, I attended midnight release parties and read the books feverishly…over and over…to my son. I posted dissertation-length theories on Mugglenet and beyond to share and connect with other fans. As an editor, I worked with Wizarding World Press to publish both *The Plot Thickens* and Book Five of the *Ultimate Unofficial Guide to the Mysteries of Harry Potter*.

What I learned through all this came together in a workshop that I presented for over a dozen years at fan, academic, and writing conferences. Together, students and I dug beneath Rowling's text to analyze the specific techniques she used to create her magic. Eventually I wrote it all down in a book to guide other writers along the way. *A Writer's Guide to Harry Potter* has recently expanded into *Teaching Harry Potter to Creative Writers: An Educator's Guide*, with more versions coming.

Engagement

The top secret that I learned through all this study on Rowling's mysteries and techniques was: Engagement! Rowling engages her fan like few other authors before or after. Her stories are more than books; they are games. She invites her reader in through quirky characters and fabulously detailed worldbuilding. Then, once trapped, she hides clues in subtext to enchant them deeper.

Rowling faithfully plays her games outside the pages of her books. Throughout interviews, premiers, and her online presence, she keeps the secrets secret and strings the clues along.

Her reward for all this: fans want to play in her world long after the book is closed and the film is on DVD. From Wizard Wrock to fanfic to fan art to theme parks, her fans just can't get enough. Now we have a new story to take apart...together.

About this Clue Book

This guide is a clue book of possibilities. I never believe that *all* my theories are true, but they are possible starting points for discussion. Rowling challenged us with a game to play...*if you've got your wits about you*. I hope you will join in. Please see *Where to Go From Here* at the end with ways to keep engaged and sleuthing until Fantastic Beasts 2.

Due to the nature of this book, **beware of spoilers**! I'm not talking only about spoilers revealing details of this first movie, either. We will peer deep into the tea leaves for what's to come for the remaining four movies.

Canon

For my purposes. I will consider anything canon that is direct from the movie, the script book, or written by JK Rowling on Pottermore. I will also give close observation to anything Rowling has said in interviews, but will note it as such.

Running Bits

"Running bits" is a term I'm borrowing from Galadriel Waters of Wizarding World Press. During the height of the Harry Potter craze, her *Ultimate Unofficial Guides to the Mysteries of Harry Potter* were the best way to discover all the secrets that eluded your first five readings.

Running bits refer to items mentioned repeatedly that point toward a key clue in that particular book or the whole series. Clocks were a running bit for *Prisoner of Azkaban*, as were frogs and water for *Chamber of Secrets*.

Within Fantastic Beasts, I've detected a few that will be discussed throughout this guide. Keep your eyes open for:

- Five
- Water
- Memories
- Blue and white
- Salem Witch Trials
- And watch out for the ghost and graves.

JK Rowling is up to her old tricks. Put on your sleuthing cap and let's get to work.

Secret One

An Occamy in a Teapot

(Worldbuilding)

For many years, Harry's wizarding world has expanded well beyond the pages of the massive books Rowling wrote for his series. We've had Pottermore direct from Rowling plus the details revealed in interviews, games, and witch and wizard cards...not to even mention the movies.

Then there's the fan expansion edition—the Wizard Wrock, the fanfic, fan art, fan theories and companion books. It all too much to take in...even before you hop aboard the Hogwarts Express to Universal's Wizarding World of Harry Potter theme park.

With *Fantastic Beasts*, however, we have the wizarding world expanding in a uniquely new and exciting way. Rowling herself is creating more of her world that does not center Harry as its focus.

Through the FB script book and film, we can search and find all the new details which makes Rowling's world such a delight for her fans to play in. Through worldbuilding both large and small, through a wide-angle lens and a zoom, she has crafted a slightly different world that is both true to what has come before while reenergizing fandom with its fresh and different spin.

The timing is historical to Harry. But not only that, this story takes place in a matter of days, not a school year. The location starts in a new country, with different laws, culture, history, and ways of viewing their No-Maj neighbors.

The institutions, city, buildings, food, drinks, and all the minute details Rowling layered into her world shows that magic lives and breathes in the US just as vibrantly as it did in the UK.

While the star characters are grown up, more sure of their purpose and direction in life, they are still Rowling's quirky, somewhat awkward, wounded heroes seeking direction to make a difference.

Through all this, the magic remains true to Rowling's original vision of a world of magic and wonder that is only diagonally separated from our own. One where we can better examine some of the conflict that grips ours through the prism of a fantasy that shows us what we could be if we viewed imagination as one of the most powerful tools we possess.

Timing

Rowling has said in interviews that the Fantastic Beasts series will span nineteen years. Nineteen years was also the amount of time between Harry Potter and the Epilogue. Nineteen years will take us to 1945, the end of WWII and the defeat of Grindelwald.

The most significant aspect to the timing of the story is WWII. As such, throughout this guide, I'll be on the lookout for any clues that relate to it. And knowing Rowling's strong voice and support for contemporary social issues, I'll note any as they correspond to today's current political climate.

While each Harry Potter book spanned the course of one school year at Hogwarts, even *Deathly Hallows* though it did not take place there, the first *Fantastic Beasts* film takes place in a few days, the bulk of it in two. On the next few pages, I have charted out what happened in each of the days.

1926

With Rowling, choices matter. Every choice she makes in sculpting her world usually serves a specific purpose. I'm sure that is true of the year she sets each film. Though we may not know for sure this early into the franchise, here are a couple of guesses for her choice of 1926:

- 1926 is the year of Voldemort's birth.
- It is also the year the second volume of Hitler's *Mein Kampf* was published.
- The year Godiva chocolates was founded.

Well, maybe not that last. But considering the powerful effect chocolate has on Dementors, I'll keep it there.

Timeline

Day	Time	Setting	Note
1	Night	Europe	Grindelwald's attack
2	Next Morning	Ship	Newt warning Dougal
	Dusk	Near City Hall subway	Obscurus attack
3	Day	Bank	Mary Lou, then Jacob
		MACUSA	With Tina —Picquery dismissal, then wand office.
		Jacob's room	Opens Newt's case.
		Second Salem Church	Pigeon scene and serving soup
	Afternoon	Newt and Tina on street	Passing a "gas" explosion
		Jacob's room	Newt and Tina enter.
		Streets of NY	Hint of Demiguise and Occamy on street and entering building.
	Dusk	Shaw Newsroom	Langdon brings in Barebones
		Tina and Queenie's apartment	Tina brings home Newt and Jacob.
	Night	Credence on street	Meeting Graves
		Goldstein apartment	Dinner with Team
		Inside Newt's case	Jacob and Newt and beasts

Day	Time	Setting	Note
3	Night	Second Salem Church	Mary Lou whips Credence.
		Diamond District	Niffler and cops
		Central Park	Erumpent on loose
		City Hall	Senator Shaw dinner. Shaw killed.
		Pentagram Office, MACUSA	International Wizards. Team arrested.
4	Day	MACUSA jail cell	Newt, Tina, Jacob, discussing Obscurial
		Second Salem Church	Children gathering pamphlets, Modesty throws hers away.
		Interrogation room	Newt and Tina before Graves
		Death Chamber	Swooping Evil to the rescue
		MACUSA	Queenie frees Newt, Tina, and Jacob
	Late Afternoon	Streets of NY	Graves meets Credence, pushing to find child.
	Dusk	Rooftop with pigeon coop	Newt and Tina and Queenie and Jacob
	Night	The Blind Pig	Gnarlak gives info on Demiguise and betrays them.

Day	Time	Setting	Note
4	Night	Second Salem Church	Credence discovers Modesty's toy wand; Obscurus kills Mary Lou, Chastity.
		Department store	Team retrieves Dougal and Occamy.
		Inside Newt's case	Team, picture of Leta
		Second Salem Church	Credence has summoned Graves.
		Tenement in Bronx, Modesty's birth home	Credence erupts.
		Squire's rooftop	Team observing Obscurus
		Times Square	Graves tries to appeal to Credence, Newt and Tina apparate in.
		Across New York	Obscurus and Newt race across rooftops.
		City Hall subway	Climax scene, Graves unveiled as Grindelwald
5	Dawn	Sky	Frank flies and releases antidote.
		Subway entrance	Jacob in rain
Week Later	Early Evening	Jacob's canning factory	Newt passes him Occamy shells.
Next Day		New York Harbor	Newt and Tina separate.
3 Months	Day	Jacob's bakery	Queenie enters.

We all know the destruction which followed from the nature of Voldemort's birth. Hitler's *Mein Kampf* set forth his political motivations against the Jewish people, including passages that promoted their emigration and extermination.[1] The book was widely popular in Germany.

We don't know yet the year in which the next film will be set, but I've included my best guesses in the Forecast chapter.

Christmas at Macy's and Pearl Harbor Date

This famous department store is chosen as the hiding place for Dougal and the Occamy. I'm wondering if this choice is simply a matter of whimsy, or if there's something more to it.

One element the Macy's location[2] helps with is the timing of the story. Although the newspaper headlines at the beginning of the film informed us the year was 1926, most viewers will not be able to catch the small print dates from the end of November to early December. However, the Christmas displays at Macy's informs us what season we're in.

Throughout Harry Potter, both in the books and with special reveals on her website, Rowling liked to time important scenes and clues with significant events, whether astronomical or historical.

In *Fantastic Beasts*, Rowling is literally starting her new series in the "dead" of winter, at a moment when the world seems to be darkening. But as you will see in the Obscurus section in the Forecast at the end, the death is not final. A wisp of Credence, of the Obscurus, survives.

However, she not only sets the first film in winter, she ties it to a very significant date in history. When one is able to see the dates of the newspapers shown during the course of the movie, you'll notice that the date when Mary Lou Barebone is killed and the Obscurus is unleashed on New York is December 7, 1926. Fifteen years later, Pearl Harbor will be attacked and the US will enter WWII.

Looking forward to the next movies, could we see each of these stories taking place around a significant period? Rowling has freed herself from the year at Hogwarts timeframe and chosen a much shorter period, at least for this first movie. Perhaps she has chosen to replace the old frame with a newer one that will hold just as much meaning. Unfortunately, we need

---

[1] https://en.wikipedia.org/wiki/Mein_Kampf#Antisemitism

[2] The film shows the store as Ginzberg Delaunay, but in the script book it is referred to as Macy's.

more than one example to prove a pattern, so we'll have to wait for more info regarding the next movie.

Wide-Angle Lens

Rowling sets her worldbuilding through both a wide-angle lens and a zoom. Through the wide angle we get the sense of the breadth of her community, one that has now expanded to the United States and New York. Many of these new places relate to their counterpart back in the UK:

- MACUSA—Ministry of Magic
- Ilvermorny—Hogwarts
- Death Pool of Memories—Death Arch
- The New York Ghost—The Daily Prophet
- The Goldstein's Apartment—The Burrow

In the next sections, we'll look at her large scale worldbuilding for the new series. Then, in the Zoom Lens below, we'll cover some of the fantastic new details.

Scourers

Scourers do not appear directly in *Fantastic Beasts*, but are instead part of its backstory, which Rowling reveals through Pottermore.

They are the American wizarding form of vigilante justice—groups of wizards who started out to protect the magical community, and, becoming increasingly corrupt, almost ended them. Scourers formed to fill the void left by the absence of magical law enforcement. However, as their power and greed grew, and facing no opposition, many turned into corrupt bounty hunters willing to traffic in both wizard and No-Maj, whether guilty or innocent. The magical community finally rallied together to wipe them out. To survive, many former Scourers married with No-Majs and sought to breed the magic out of their line…though not the knowledge.

The purpose of the Scourers, as I see it, is to serve as a replacement for the Pureblood ideology of the Potter series. Just as in the No-Maj world, wizard nobility did not transfer across the ocean. It was instead replaced with a stronger distrust and separation between the magical and human world. One built on betrayal from within.

We know that Mary Lou has Scourer heritage due to her surname Barebone. Bartholomew Barebone, a No-Maj descended from Scourers, suckered witch Dorcus Twelvetrees into giving him her wand, which he then displayed to reporters, causing a huge breach of magical secrecy.

Because of this, the wizarding community in the US went even more underground and the separation between wizards and No-Maj became even more distrustful…on both sides.

Thus, the Scourers reign of terror set up Mary Lou's Second Salem thread and the very divisive situation Newt encounters in New York. One that hints at the nationalism which is about to grip the world.

I'm guessing that at some point in time we'll hear more about magical historian Theophilius Abbot and his tracking of families descended from Scourers. Perhaps he has written a book about them!

Salem Witch Trials

The Salem Witch Trials are repeatedly hinted at throughout the screenplay, serving as a running bit. Most prominent is Mary Lou Barebone's organization, the New Salem Philanthropic Society, commonly referred to as the Second Salemers. They make their home in an old church, The Second Salem Church. In this religious imagery, I sense a sly reference to the Second Coming, setting up an apocalyptic theme of the story (see the Theme chapter for more). However, there are a couple of other subtle references to the witch trials.

Tina uses two exclamations that are names of women involved in the trials:

1) Deliverance Dane – one of the women accused of witchcraft -- used as an exclamation by Tina when she asks Newt why he let the Niffler loose.

2) Mercy Lewis – one of the accusers – Tina utters this one in Jacob's apartment when the creatures escaped.

Then there are Modesty's dolls. We see these in Scene 84 in Modesty's bedroom, all lined up. One has a noose tied around its neck while the other is tied to a stake. In the Salem witch trials, all but one of the twenty people sentenced to death were executed by hanging.

With Modesty having another doll tied to a stake, could we perhaps see the Inquisition form a role in future movies?

Most of what we know about Salem's influence on American magical history comes by way of Rowling's pre-film writing for Pottermore. In her "History of Magic in North America" series, she shares two important repercussions from the Salem Witch Trials:

1) As news spread back to Europe regarding the trials, few Purebloods chose to migrate to America. Since more witches and

wizards were born of No-Maj families proportionally, Americans did not develop the prejudice of Pureblood as in the old countries.

2) Because of the terror caused by the trials and the Scourers, the magical community came together to form their own government—the Magical Congress of the United States of America (MACUSA).

Rowling developed this backstory for a purpose. The confines of a script are much tighter than that of a 750-page book. With both the printing of the script book and the history she released beforehand, she sought to give her fans an extra hand in puzzling out her clues.

One of these clues I think she hopes we will piece together is the connection between the Scourers, the Salem Witch Trials, and Mary Lou's New Salemers.

All believe in magic. And all seek to wipe it out.

Whereas Voldemort's war was based on purity of blood, a conflict largely based within the magical world, Rowling seems to be pitching for a wider conflict with this story. Based on the history of the Scourers and Mary Lou's Second Salemers, Rowling may very well be setting up a world war scenario that will pit the entire wizarding world against all No-Maj.

MACUSA

The Magical Congress of the United States of America (MACUSA) is the governing body of the wizarding community in the US. Located in New York City inside the Woolworth building, MACUSA operates as an extension with hundreds of stories within the No-Maj structure. An owl carved over the entrance to the building marks it as a secret wizarding facility.

MACUSA was founded because of the Salem Witch Trials and the trouble caused by the Scourers (see those sections above for more). Its history has been fraught with moves and scandals as it has sought increasingly to separate and hide from the No-Maj community who caused American witches and wizards such harm. As such, the current president tolerates no breaches of security whatsoever.

We see within the MACUSA leadership the same ambiguity of power that was within the Ministry of Magic. While President Picquery seems sincerely intent on protecting the magical community, she is also willing to exterminate a disturbed young man who could have been helped instead of killed.

Rowling wrote a detailed history of MACUSA, which you can find on Pottermore. With time, I will explore more links between the background of MACUSA and our current story through my BeastChaser.com blog. Please share any insights you have there.

MACUSA-Specific Laws

Magical government is not the same in the US as it is in the UK, and there are a few different laws to show this point:

- No breeding of magical creatures in NY
- Foreigners must apply for a wand permit.
- No witch or wizard can friend or marry a No-Maj

It's this last one that is most likely to show up as a problem through the rest of the series, especially between Queenie and Jacob. Also, if we're about to do an around-the-world tour, I'll be curious to see the variety of laws we encounter.

Ilvermorny School of Witchcraft and Wizardry

Ilvermorny sets up an interesting contrast to Hogwarts. Where Hogwarts was founded by four of the most magical witches and wizards of their age, Ilvermorny was founded by one family. However, this family was made up of different types of people. There were two adopted sons, a No-Maj immigrant and a Pureblood immigrant, and then their daughters. We could also consider a founder in a magical being, the Pukwudgie. Even though it was one family, they had very diverse components.

The school does not play a prominent role in the movie, although quite an extensive history is given on Pottermore. Ilvermorny is mentioned once by Queenie, which prompts Newt to counter that Hogwarts is better.

In the Theme chapter, I cover the important theme of an inclusive society which Rowling's backstory builds. Here, I'll focus on the make-up of the four Houses.

I consider this chart a starting point. As we find out more about Ilvermorny and the other wizarding schools going forward, some of this information may prove useful.

We know that Madam Picquery was in the Horned Serpent House, but have not (at this point) been informed of any others. I'd guess Tina was in Wampus and Queenie in Pukwudgie.

Ilvermorny House	Founder	Student Character	Element	Body
Thunderbird	Chadwick Boot, Wizard	Adventurers	Air	Soul
Wampus	Webster Boot, Wizard	Warriors	Earth	Body
Horned Serpent	Isolt Sayre, Pureblood	Scholars	Water	Mind
Pukwudgie	James Steward, No-Maj	Healers	Fire	Heart

I'll add more to this chart on my blog at HarryPotterForWriters.com as we find out more information about the houses.

International Confederation of Wizards

In a room designed like an "old parliament debating chamber," (p. 143), Madam Picquery meets with a delegation of witches and wizards from around the world. Apparently, they are the International Confederation of Wizards mentioned previously as threatening to send a delegation.

Tina enters the scene unaware of the ramifications as she brings Newt's suitcase before Madam Picquery. The exact location of where she thumps on Newt's case, opening it to reveal Newt and Jacob, is discussed under Pentagram in the Myths chapter. What I wish to do in this section is to analyze the foreign witches and wizards we meet.

This scene is crucial to setting up the series going forward. If Rowling is preparing for a world war that spans both Wizards and No-Maj at war, she must show some of these actors from the start, even if they do not play a significant role in this current story.

The next page is a table of speaking characters in the Pentagram Office scene and hints we can divine from their presence.

The central aspect of this scene is the hologram of Senator Shaw's body floating above the gathering. When Madam Ya Zhou asks Newt which one of his creatures did this, Newt instantly shoots back "No creature did this...Don't pretend!" (p. 147). He's accusing the gathering of *pretending* not to know that it was an Obscurus who attacked and killed Senator Shaw.

Character	Country of Origin (Guess)	Dialogue	Hints for Future
Heinrich Eberstadt	Switzerland	"Our American friends have permitted a breach of the Statute of Secrecy…" (p. 143)	Switzerland was supposedly neutral during WWII, but in reality conducted trade or attacked planes on either side as benefited their economy and safety. With the largest percentage of the population speaking Swiss German, plus with Eberstadt's words a carefully constructed diplomatic attack on the MACUSA president, I predict this character will play a large role in the series.
Madam Picquery	USA	As the officiator, speaks throughout. Accuses Eberstadt of letting Grindelwald slip through his fingers. Criticizes Tina for disrupting the meeting, and then attacks her for not reporting sooner. Denies the existence of an Obscurial in the US, then orders Newt and the others to be arrested.	At this point in the story, Picquery appears to be a smarter version of Fudge. While she seems sincere in her intent to protect the secrecy of the magical community, she is also opposed to our team and blinded to the reality of the existence of an Obscurial. Via Pottermore, we know her term of office ends in 1928. May the end of her presidency play a role in the next story?
British Envoy (unnamed, probably because we'd recognize the surname)	England	Recognizes Newt, who greets him as "Minister." Recognizes instantly that Newt's cover story to buy the Puffskein is a lie.	Obviously is personally familiar with Newt and a member of the Ministry of Magic. In referring to Newt as Theseus' "little" brother rather than "younger," seems to deprecate him. Quite sure he'll play a role, but not sure it will be one of assistance.
Momolu Wotorson	Possibly Liberia or Ethiopia	Mistakes Newt for his brother Theseus, the war hero.	The biggest hint I see here is that the story will possibly take a turn in Africa.
Madam Ya Zhou	China (though her name is literally the Chinese word for *Asia*, as in the Asian continent)	Asks Newt which of his creatures was responsible for Senator Shaw's death.	A trip to Asia is probably in our forecast as well

While Madam Picquery quickly denies the possibility, I'm reminded of Fudge's refusal to accept the return of Voldemort. Is this horror just too much for these wizarding world leaders to comprehend? Or is it politically disadvantageous for them to acknowledge that an Obscurus at full power exists?

Finally, this scene presents us with the strongest evidence to this point where Rowling may be headed for locations in the remaining four films. With the African and Asian delegate given speaking roles, it contributes to my belief that Rowling's series may span five continents (see Forecast chapter). If there's one thing that seems for certain, Rowling is setting this new series against an international backdrop as compared to Harry's British one.

Zoom Lens

Rowling excels at fleshing out the minute details of worldbuilding that her fans so delight in. But this is a greater challenge in a script than in a novel. Scripts are more limited in words and space. Plus, many of the details are handled by the huge crew that creates the film as a team. Usually, a novelist builds her world from her one imagination (perhaps in consultations with her support team).

Therefore, the most significant details in the zoom lens of *Fantastic Beasts* are the ones specifically mentioned in the script book, because we know these are the ones Rowling planned herself.

In the sections below, we'll look at this wonderful new detail for clues as to the series' hidden mysteries and what's still to come.

Magical Reads and Bubbly Brews

Fantastic Beasts is not filled with as much juicy detail in the form of food and books as the Harry Potter series, but there are a few I'd like to mention and keep track of. The reason I highlight the food and the books is because Rowling has used both in the past to hide important clues.

For food, we have the magical strudel that Queenie whips up which so delights Jacob. Later, Jacob quickly develops a fondness for gigglewater, an alcoholic drink that makes you giggle after you drink it. I loved this one.

In terms of books and magazines, a few are mentioned, both in the film and in the supporting backstory on Pottermore.

- *Big Foot's Last Stand* by Ortiz O'Flaherty (mentioned in The New York Ghost)
- *Chadwick's Charms*—Spellbook used at Ilvermorny

- *The Flap of the Cape* by Abigail R. Cankus—seen in the Goldstein apartment
- *The Owl Airforce* by Simon Detanta—seen in the Goldstein apartment.
- *The Witch's Friend*—magazine in the Goldstein apartment
- *Witch Chat*—magazine in the Goldstein apartment
- *Transfiguration Today*—magazine in the Goldstein apartment
- *Cassandra and Her Cat Gustavus*—book Jacob is reading in the Goldstein apartment

Of these books, the one that intrigues me the most is *Transfiguration Today*. Not only does the copy that appears on screen talk about unregistered animagi (above an article contributed by Albus Dumbledore, on Metamorphagus—see section on Dumbledore for more), but the fact that it's inside the Goldstein apartment hints at my animagi theory regarding Tina (see the Plot chapter for more).

The other intriguing books is *The Owl Airforce*. With a war in the future that will be fought largely in the air, I worry for the poor owls.

One more question about the books so far—I wonder if we may be headed for a "last stand" scenario by series end? A last stand is military strategy where a less powerful group stands their ground against a much more powerful force, knowing they will likely not survive but may still strategically help their side.

Wandmakers from Pottermore

While none of the wands are described specifically by Rowling in the script book, she has given us some information via Pottermore (quotes from Pottermore).

Notice the animals listed under the Core. Each has a related natural element:

- Thunderbird = Air
- Wampus Cat = Fire (a legend of the Wampus cat involves a campfire)
- White River Monster = Water
- Rougarou = Earth.

Maker	Wood	Core	Known For	Famous Owner
Shikoba Wolfe, Choctaw	Intricately carved	Tail feathers from the Thunderbird (discussed in Beasts chapter)	"Extremely powerful, though difficult to master." Preferred by Transfigurers	
Johannes Jonker, Muggleborn	Contained mother-of-pearl inlay	Wampus cat hair (discussed under Ilvermorny above)	Prized for the beauty of the mother-of-pearl.	Queenie (in movie, appears to have mother-of-pearl
Thiago Quintano	Sleek and lengthy	White River Monsters of Arkansas spine (a large river creature)	Known for "producing spells of force and elegance."	
Violetta Beauvais, New Orleans	Swamp mayhaw wood	Rougarou hair, a monster with a dog head, often linked to the werewolf.	Her wands "took to Dark magic like vampires to blood."	Seraphina Picquery

Personally, I'll be on the lookout for an intricately carved wand in the movies as I believe there is an animagi lurking about.

The Blind Pig

The Blind Pig is a speakeasy, a place that sold illegal alcohol during the Prohibition era. These places were also called a blind pig or a blind tiger. Housed in a basement apartment accessed through a back alley, Rowling's blind pig is the dark, seedy place where New York's magical lowlifes gather.

A poster of a simpering debutante hides the entry door, reminiscent of the Fat Lady hiding the Gryffindor entrance, and wanted posters of many of the customers are proudly displayed within.

Rowling uses this scene to show us many of the magical world she'd created for the Potter series.

Magical Beings Present:

- Goblin jazz singer
- Goblin musicians
- Gnarlak—Goblin
- House-elf bartender
- House-elf servers
- Giant

Even here, across the pond, the divisions between Goblin and House-Elf are preserved, with the House-Elves in server positions and the Goblins making the money.

One final thought—the Blind Pig reminds me of the cantina on Tatooine where we first met Han Solo. But in Rowling's case, Jacob shot first.

Jazz Singer's Song

Pottermore revealed that the song the "glamorous goblin" sings in the Blind Pig was written by Rowling. As such, it deserves our attention. In my prior book, *A Writer's Guide to Harry Potter*, I analyzed Celestina Warbeck's song in "A Very Frosty Christmas" chapter of *Half-Blood Prince* for clues that led to Voldemort's Horcruxes. Let's see what this jazz singer may have hidden here:

The **phoenix** cried fat tears of pearl

When the **dragon** snapped up his best girl,

And the **Billywig** forgot to twirl

When his sweetheart left him cold,

And the **unicorn** done lost his horn,

And the **Hippogriff** feels all forlorn,

'Cause their lady loves have upped and gawn,

Or that's what I've been told— (p. 190)

Yes, love has set the beasts astir,

The dang'rous and the meek concur,

It's ruffled feathers, fleece, and fur,

'Cause love drives all of us wild. (p. 194)

Note: the bolding is mine.

Rowling weaves the song around five magical beasts losing their lady loves. With "feathers, fleece, and fur" flying, the beasts are in an uproar. While the jazz singer attributes it to the pain of love, I'm wondering if there might be another aspect at play.

With the dangers of an Obscurus wreaking havoc, and the dark wizard Grindelwald running loose, there would be a lot to frighten both wizard and beast alike. However, in this story Newt uses one beast as a weapon to wipe out the memories of a city-full of people. We've also seen the power of Swooping Evil. And don't forget how upset Pickett was when he thought Newt was willing to use him to obtain information. Could Newt's beasts hold more in store for a world about to go to war? (For more on this theory, see the Holocaust and Atomic Bomb section in the Forecast chapter.)

One aspect I'll be watching out for—to see if each of these five (there's that number again!) beasts mentioned in the song play a significant role in the series.

New Words

Here are a few new words Rowling created for this story:

- MACUSA—Magical Congress of the United States of America
- No-Maj—No Magic, the American version of Muggle
- Choranaptyxic—the ability of the Occamy to fill the space it inhabits. "Chora" comes from ancient Greek Khora meaning receptacle. See discussion on being or nonbeing. Tyxia means to pour.
- Gigglewater—an alcoholic beverage the witches and wizards drink. Makes you giggle when you drink it.

Love the name gigglewater. It makes me giggle to just say it.

New Spells

Rowling treats the reader to a few new spells in this movie.

- *Finestra* – used to shatter the glass of the jewelry store where the Niffler is in.
- *Aberto* – when Queenie tries to open Graves' office.
- The spell creates a sticky jelly which traps the Niffler on the jewelry store window
- The spell shoots out a whip of "supernatural light" at Grindelwald near the end, making him lose balance and drop his wand.

Then there are the unnamed spells in electric blue and white shot at Credence as the Obscurus in the end. These killing spells seem to be a repeat of the one seen at the very beginning of the movie.

"A sudden explosion of pure white light" (p. 1)—that's how Rowling describes the killing curse that Grindelwald shoots at the Aurors in Scene 1. We know the *Avada Kedavra* curse shoots green light. What is this spell Grindelwald uses? Is it specifically designed, like a bomb, to kill multiple people at once?

The glass shattering spell worries me considering that we may see it used by wizards in Germany during *Kristallnacht* (the Night of Shattering Glass in which Jewish businesses were destroyed in Germany in 1938). And a spell that can kill multiple people at once is even more terrifying, knowing how World War II ended.

Dolmens

I literally jumped in my seat when I saw the dolmen pictured in Newt's case. A dolmen is a megalithic structure, usually Neolithic, with upright stones topped with a large capstone. Sometimes these are called portal tombs because they were originally covered with earth or smaller stones to form a chamber (or more) with an entrance window or door. Thousands of examples still exist across Africa, Asia, and Europe.

What does the dolmen signify? Could it be a hint of something to come? I don't want to dig too deeply into the dolmen as it has only been viewed briefly inside Newt's case and may not play a significant role, but it hints to me of three themes Rowling has played with before: time, death, and a spiritual awareness.

With such a brief show of the dolmen in the movie, and no mention of it at all in the script book, this reference may not amount to anything. But I'll be on the lookout in the movies to come.

Looking Forward

Drawing upon the old, Rowling has advanced boldly into the new. Even if she went back in time to do it.

Through both the wide lens and the zoom, Rowling has increased her wizarding world to frame a new, internationally-set story, while also providing new and fun places for her fans to play. As we know the next four movies will advance into even more new locations, we're sure to have a grand tour ahead.

We must be on the lookout for each piece of worldbuilding Rowling creates. Because if there's one thing for certain, especially with the condensed form a film script allows, she will be utilizing every element allotted to her to build her story and themes while hinting at her secrets and mysteries.

Secret Two

Bound To Return

(Themes)

Themes are the glue that hold a story together. A theme is also the emotional force that makes a movie resonate with the viewer…or not. With Rowling, there are usually multiple themes at play.

Here are a few that I noticed which I feel will impact the series going forward.

Exploitation and Abuse of Children

Rowling's passion, outside her novels, is to advocate for children's welfare, especially those who have no one to advocate for them. She established her Lumos foundation to provide a voice for these who often go unheard. Through villains such as Dolores Umbridge and Mary Lou Barebone, Rowling shows there is no one more detestable than those who use and abuse children.

Within *Fantastic Beasts*, we meet the unfortunate Barebone children. Though Chastity and Credence are described now as adults, they, along with Modesty, spent their formative years being exploited and abused by Mary Lou. Credence's abuse continues beyond the Barebone home. Graves/Grindelwald manipulates his desire to be cherished and loved for his own good. And even Madam Picquery, charged with protecting all wizardkind, determines to kill this young, wounded wizard rather than to try and save him.

Even beyond the Barebones, there is the sense other characters were wounded as children. Langdon Shaw strives so hard to please his father because he knows his brother is the favored one. And Newt, living in the adows of his own war-hero brother, should never have been expelled from Hogwarts for his noble loyalty to a friend.

For Rowling, abusing or neglecting a child is such a devastating human force, resulting in injury not only to the child, but our society as a whole, that it could only be shown in the raw hurricane-like destruction of the Obscurus. But like the life-giving rains of the hurricane, the Obscurial's power can create rather than destroy. Think of what could be accomplished in the real world if the repressed energy and talents of all children were nurtured in a loving home environment.

Finally, it is worth noting that Grindelwald also recognizes the power in these children left behind. He recognizes the benefit of putting their wasted creative talents to his service. He merely does not possess the ability to recognize the power when abuse has cloaked it in weakness until it is too late.

Redefining Slytherin

Neither Slytherin nor Gryffindor are mentioned within Fantastic Beasts. After all, Hogwarts is not the focus of this new story. Only Hufflepuff is given a brief nod through Newt's scarf as that is his House.

However, in "Ilvermorny School of Witchcraft and Wizardry" provided on Pottermore before the movie's release, Slytherin had a starring role…and a surprising one.

Isolt Sayre, the founder of the North American school of Magic, Ilvermorny, was a descendant of Slytherin and a very loving and caring witch. She carried with her Slytherin's wand, which she stole when she fled from her murderous and abusive aunt, Gormlaith Gaunt. When Gormlaith finally caught up to Isolt, and was eventually defeated, Isolt buried Slytherin's wand, determined not to carry on Slytherin's legacy. However, from this broken wand grew a snakewood tree with leaves used in medicine for healing.

Isolt's chosen family portrays every union we've been told Slytherin opposed. The Sayre-Steward family consisted of a No-Maj husband, two adopted magical boys, two girls of their birth, one a witch and one a Squib, and an honorary Pukwudgie.

Isolt is a living (historical) example that good is a matter of choice and not of heritage. The choice to accept people unlike us leads to powerful magic.

Inclusive Society

As mentioned above, the founding family of Ilvermorny included a Pureblood, a No-Maj, a Half-Blood, a Squib, and an honorary magical Being.

Unlike Hogwarts, Ilvermorny was integrated within its founders. The Hogwarts Founding Four did not include a Muggle nor a Being. Beings in the UK are not even permitted to carry a wand. Where Hogwarts only looked to witches and wizards for their founding heritage, that was not the case in the USA. *Was* being the key word here.

Due to the extreme persecution of the magical community through first the Scourers and then the Salem Witch Trials, the Americans have become more segregated. More insular.

I believe this theme of inclusiveness versus nationalism will be a key theme going forward, especially considering the nature of WWII. No-Majs, witches, wizards, and magical beings and creatures must join their forces to achieve the power capable of stopping the evil they are fighting against, both without and within.

Which is why our Team from the very start already includes a No-Maj and a trunk full of beasts.

Memory

Memory is a strong theme and running bit throughout this movie. First, there is the obsession with wiping No-Maj memories. We hear about it constantly.

Perhaps one of the eeriest uses of memory is in the death chamber scene. The executioner extracts memories from Tina's head and throws them into the pool, where they show against the waters, enchanting Tina to watch, mesmerized. When the executioner's wand drops into the water, the memories turn from good to bad.

At the end we have the Swooping Evil venom potion that the Thunderbird spreads to remove all No-Maj memories of the event with the Obscurus. The film and script book shows quite clearly that the memories are washed away in the water (for more, see below).

This may be leading up to a massive memory loss of the whole planet. I can't imagine what could be more horrendous than the Holocaust or atomic bomb that Rowling will need to wipe from all our minds. But when we can't remember, history repeats itself. So, look for parallels to today.

For now, this film ends on a happy note, for there is the memory of a lover's kiss that brings a smile to Jacob's face.

Water

Starting with Newt's arrival onboard a ship, water played a large role in this story. In one of the biggest chase scenes, the Erumpent charges after Jacob and slides across a frozen lake in Central Park. Then there is the "square pool of rippling potion" (p. 163) inside the execution chamber.

Then there is the rain of the Thunderbird. We get a brief glimpse of this inside Newt's case when we first meet Frank. But the magnificence of the Thunderbird shines through when he carries the Swooping Evil venom into the storm clouds to spread the obliviating memory potion throughout the city.

It's as if the whole city is baptized at once.

If Rowling is planning on one of each of these movies representing the five recesses of the pentagram (see section on Pherecydes in the Myth chapter), this this movie would definitely be water.

Apocalypse

There is also an apocalyptic strain that runs through *Fantastic Beasts*. This fear of end times is heightened with such mentions as the Second Salemers and their end-times message, which hints at the Second Coming.

Also, in the name Barebone, there is the link to the Fifth Monarchists. This is a seventeenth century religious sect that based their apocalyptic thinking on a passage from the book of Daniel, which prophesied four kingdoms passing away before the fifth would reign in the Kingdom of God. They were awaiting the Fifth Monarch to reign in the Second Coming, which they believed would happen in 1666.

Praise-God Barebone was one of the movement's leaders.

When a community feels its very existence is threatened, apocalyptic thinking and literature become prevalent. With the approaching world war, people will feel their existence threatened even more.

In Rowling's story, there are two communities which will be feeling the pains of apocalyptic fears—both the wizarding and the No-Maj. Which is not good for either side, for as Madam Picquery stated:

...when No-Majs are afraid, they attack. (p. 42)

With Grindelwald intent on bringing about a "mass slaughter for the greater good" (p. 158), we're sure both wizard and No-Maj alike will be very, very afraid.

Secret Three

Like Doxys Among Us

(Characters)

With JK Rowling, a story starts with a person. A person who comes into her mind, like Harry did on that famous train trip in 1991, with a story she cannot forget. And only she can tell.

In an interview at the New York City premiere for *Fantastic Beasts and Where to Find Them*, Rowling said that this exciting new story in her familiar wizarding world started with Newt.

"Newt just lodged in my head and I just knew more about Newt than I needed to know. And that's always a good sign because that was organic—that just happened....So I basically set down to write what I knew about Newt and that led us here, because I ended up writing the screenplay."[3]

What story does Newt have to share that fascinated Rowling? And what element makes it necessary for *five* movies? It's my mission to delve into these mysteries. Using what I have learned from years of studying the Harry Potter series, let's dig beneath her script's surface and I'll reveal some of the very sly clues she has hidden to tease of what is to come.

---

[3]   https://www.pottermore.com/news/jk-rowling-attends-fantastic-beasts-world-premiere-in-new-york

Overview:

Characters we'll examine:

Newt Scamander	Porpentina Goldstein
Queenie Goldstein	Jacob
The Team	Percival Graves
Grindelwald	Credence Barebones
Mary Lou Barebones	Chastity Barebones
Modesty Barebones	Serephina Picquery
Shaw father	Shaw senator
Shaw son	Bingley
Other guy in bank	Other guy in ministry
Lestrange	Dumbledore and his family
Newt's older brother	

Newton Artemis Fido Scamander

The first thing we need to understand about Newt is that he is a Magizoologist. He's a scientist. I believe this will be crucial going forward into the series. From the moment he steps into the alien world of New York City, he observes it with a "scientist's curiosity" (p. 9).

"Weather-beaten, wiry, wearing an old blue overcoat" (p. 2), Newt reminds me of my favorite Defense Against the Dark Arts professor, Lupin. Newt seems battered and weary, like Lupin, perhaps from having traveled among some of the worst of his species. People whom he considers "the most vicious creatures on the planet" (p. 113).

Note, too, that the color of the overcoat was important enough to mention specifically in the script (see the White and Blue section in the Plot chapter). He was also expelled from Hogwarts for endangering student life with a beast, as I will cover in the Shipping chapter.

Newt
I annoy people. (p. 121)

More comfortable among his beasts than humans, Newt comes across as awkward and is hesitant to get to know those he meets. Jacob wins Newt's friendship when he shelters his Occamy egg. When they journey inside Newt's case, and Jacob marvels at his beasts, Newt delights to Jacob's interest, like any proud parent would.

With her natural Legilimency, Queenie arouses his scientific interest. However, when she understands his pain and protects the secret knowledge her Legilimency gives of him, she wins his respect.

And Tina...Tina wins his heart when he sees in her memories that she would sacrifice herself for the least of humans, just as he would for the least of animals. She then turns that same attention to saving his Demiguise and Occamy.

The moment from Newt that touched my heart the most was his pleading for the safety of his beasts when his own life was imperiled:

Newt
(screaming, desperate)

Don't hurt those creatures— there is nothing in there that is dangerous. Please don't hurt my creatures— they are not dangerous . . . Please, they are not dangerous! (p. 149)

Newt loves his creatures and will do anything to protect them. He's a true conservationist.

Like Harry, Newt comes across as a bit insecure. However, Newt *is* secure in his mission. He knows these animals, he loves and understands them, and he is determined to protect them at all costs.

With Rowling, the name of a character tells us quite a bit about his nature and role in the story. Newt's name gives us a lot to go on.

Let us assume that Newton refers to Sir Isaac Newton. Besides being one of the most famous scientists of all time, Newton was equally fascinated with alchemy; a fascination he shares with Rowling.

Some of Newton's experiments produced what alchemists called the Tree of Diana – a metal substance that appeared to grow on the vial in the shape of a tree. Perhaps it is this that links *Newton* to the *Artemis* part of Newt's name, as the Greek Artemis was Diana in Rome. Artemis was the Mistress of Animals and, in Ephesus where her famous temple stood, was particularly associated with stags and bees.

I find it interesting that two of Newt's names link him strongly to Anatolia, which is modern day Turkey. The Temple of Artemis stood in Ephesus. The river Scamander and the god associated with it were near Troy. For more on this connection, see the Myth chapter under Trojan War.

A few other points to note about Newt:

- He's a proud Hufflepuff, as shown by the scarf in his luggage at customs that he also wears at the end.
- With all the beasts and various things he pulls out of his blue coat, he reminds me of Hagrid. I wonder if he was Hagrid's mentor.

- In WWI, he worked on the Eastern Front with dragons. Ukrainian Ironbellies sound like tanks.

- In his willingness to hand over Pickett to Gnarlak, while knowing that he'd retrieve his Bowtruckle as soon as possible, Newt shows that he is not the pushover he may appear to be.

- Finally, there was a deleted shirtless scene showing Newt's scarring from all the beasts he's worked with.

Porpentina Esther Goldstein

Tina wants to appear important and in control, but her awkwardness keeps tripping her up. She's the "career girl" according to her sister Queenie, but she threw her position away because she cared more about protecting a young man from abuse. In this, she is a perfect match for Newt, which will be discussed more in the Shipping chapter.

Queenie sometimes calls her sister Teenie. This could just be a play on their names together: Queenie and Teenie, but I think there might be something more there. A hint perhaps. (See Animagi section in the Plot chapter). Orphaned since their parents died of dragon pox, the sisters only have each other. They share a strong bond, which helps save Tina and Newt's life from the death chamber.

As for her name: Goldstein has alchemy links. In German, it means gold stone, which is a reference to alchemy. It's also a common Jewish name, which considering the nature of the series, probably hints at their Jewish heritage.

Porpentina may refer to the Porpentine Inn, which was an inn in Shakespeare's *Comedy of Errors*. This comedy is based on a series of misunderstandings and misfortunate events based on the mix-ups between two sets of twins. As Rowling thought of Tina's name long before she developed the plot for the movies, it may or may not play a significant role.

Esther, however, her middle name, is something new. Most likely it's a link to the ancient Queen Esther, a Jewish woman in exile and another hint at the Goldstein sister's Jewish history. For more on Esther, see *Queenie* below.

Queenie Goldstein

> "...the most beautiful girl ever to don witches' robes"
> (p. 79).

The first thing you note about Queenie, aside from her beauty, is that she is warm and loving…and incredibly straight forward. She has a delightful way of talking that puts you in mind of the new talkie film stars of the 1920s.

Queenie reminds me a bit of Luna Lovegood, in a delightful way. She's got a hint of that offbeat quirkiness that we love about Luna but in a more practical manner. She wields her Legilimency with empathy and sincere interest. So, even though someone like Newt may object to having his mind read, he doesn't protest the way Queenie does it. Her ability with Legilimency has already saved the lives of Newt and Tina. I'm sure it will continue to be incredibly useful going forward.

As for her name, I believe Queenie goes together with Tina's middle name, Esther, to point us toward Queen Esther and her book in the Hebrew Bible (Old Testament). This is the story of a Jewish woman chosen to become queen in Persia. When the king's Grand Vizier, Haman, perceives a slight to his own pride from a Jew refusing to bow to him, he goes before the king proclaiming the Jews to be worthless and vowing to pay a huge sum if the king will allow him to eradicate them all. The king issues an order for all the Jews to be killed and their property confiscated. (You can clearly see the parallels to WWII). Esther risks her own life to plead with the king to save theirs. Haman is instead hung on the gallows he erected to kill her people.

As such, I would expect to see Queenie and Tina work together to save many Jews from the death camps. I just hope Queenie doesn't lose her own life doing so.

Jacob Kowalski

Jacob wants to make people happy, and he does, fans included. The only No-Maj among this team of wizard and witches, Jacob proves himself to be more than helpful.

Before he even knows Newt well, he guards the Occamy egg in the bank, returning the hatchling safely to its guardian. As with the Occamy, he notices things Newt misses, such as closing Newt's case when he's off chasing the Niffler. Jacob breaks down Graves' door when Queenie's spells don't work. And when he knocks Gnarlak out, we all cheered. I have a bit of a hard time imagining Newt using this type of brute force.

Jacob returned from WWI in 1924. He was part of the Expeditionary Forces, as he indicates…digging. Now he's working in a canning factory, and as he says, dying.

Jacob

That's why I want to make pastries, you know. It makes people happy. (p. 122)

No way do I think the choice of Baker is happenstance for Jacob. With Rowling, every choice has meaning. Jacob wants to make people happy.

But it's not just that. He says he's dying working in the factory, everyone is. It is also about giving life. Jacob is a life giver.

He also, by hint of his surname and his grandmother's recipe, seems to be of Polish descent. In Polish, *Kowal* means Smith, and the *pączki* that Jacob shows off to the banker is a Polish doughnut.

Poland is no accidental choice either. The invasion of Poland by Nazi forces in 1939 set off WWII.

Rowling said in an interview that Jacob is like Ron, especially I assume in regard to his loyalty, but I also see a bit of Neville in this character. Neville was initially an outsider due to his lack of magical power. As a No-Maj, Jacob has none. He does, however, come into his own brand of power based on his practicality, as mentioned above.

One hint I'd *like* to see with Jacob, but not sure that it's more than wishful thinking, is a possible link to Jacob of the Hebrew Bible (Old Testament), especially regarding the story of Jacob's ladder. Here is why it's wishful thinking: Jacob was the father of a new nation. Jacob's ladder showed a pathway or connection with the divine that brought a promise for Jacob's descendants.

If Rowling is hinting at this ancient story (and I admit I'm grasping a bit here), it could be a promise that Jacob, and Queenie, will come out of this all right and start a new dynasty in America that circles back to its beginning: a harmonious marriage between witch and No-Maj.

One little tidbit in support of this theory…when Jacob descends the first time into Newt's case, once he gets past the stuck part at least, it seems he's going down a ladder.

One can hope!

The Team

One theme which we saw strongly portrayed throughout Harry Potter was the power of friendship. For Harry, it was a hard lesson to learn, but he finally come to grasp that what he couldn't do alone, he *could* do with the help of his friends.

Rowling continues this important team experience in *Fantastic Beasts*, and we're starting to see the skills and personality each person brings to the group.

Tina is an Auror and possible Animagi (see the section in the Plot chapter). She will have a powerful ability to protect the team going forward. **Queenie** is a Legilimens. Her skills at mind reading will be incredibly beneficial. **Newt** knows and understands the animals that may be the primary focus of Grindelwald going forward. And that leaves **Jacob**. What will he have to offer?

Jacob has already shown himself to be a very practical and powerful help. From breaking down Graves' office door to regain Newt's case to slugging Gnarlak, Jacob has already proven himself a valuable member of the team. But I think Jacob's greatest contribution will be the happiness he brings to his friends…and not only through his pastries.

As for personality of the team—Newt's calm and inquisitive nature is in direct contrast to Harry who had been taught by the Dursleys never to ask questions. We must remember that while Harry was a youth discovering himself, Newt is an adult who has found his way in the world. This story is set on a different dynamic.

Although Rowling has likened Jacob to Ron in loyalty, I see these characters as very different. Jacob seems more secure in his purpose in life, and without five older brothers to live up to, is less likely to feel in Newt's shadow.

Teenie and Queenie are a lovely pair. Queenie's unabashed interest in the people around her and warm, quixotic personality contrasts her sister's shyer and awkward reserve. However, together they provide a safe home and understanding for these two men who both seem a bit lost and wandering.

Rowling is noted for her quirky characters. In Fantastic Beasts, her leads seem to have taken on a charming hint of awkwardness as well…except for Queenie. Rowling has said in interviews that her heroes are "always people who feel themselves to be set apart, stigmatized, or othered."[4] We get that sense here with each of her team members.

---

[4]   http://comicbook.com/2016/11/08/ezra-miller-hints-at-who-plays-grindelwald-in-fantastic-beasts-a/

Percival Graves

As we never see the true Percival Graves in the movie, I'm covering most of this character in the Grindelwald section below. However, as Grindelwald presented himself in such a way as to be recognized as Graves, we can assume a few things about the Auror.

As the head Auror for MACUSA, Graves must be a very skilled and accomplished wizard. He seems to have earned the respect of Madam Picquery and the staff. Abernathy is particularly deferential to him. Graves is also a descendant of Gondulphus Graves, one of the original twelve Aurors for MACUSA.

For his first name, my hunch is that it is a link to Dumbledore (for more see the Dumbledore section). Regarding the surname, I'm intrigued by the possible link to Leslie Groves, the director of The Manhattan Project, responsible for developing the atomic bomb. As you will see from my discussion in the Forecast chapter, I think this link will be key throughout the series.

Rowling likes to hide a villain within each story, and Graves provided the perfect cover for Grindelwald. In the Plot chapter, under Clues, I have a section which lists the heads-up Rowling gave us regarding the secret nature of Graves.

How Grindelwald became Graves is never presented, but we can assume via Polyjuice Potion as we saw the same feat successfully accomplished by Barty Crouch, Jr. nearly seventy years later.

As we know through Barty, Graves would probably still need to be alive and nearby so that Grindelwald could harvest his hairs or toenail clippings. Ugh. This leaves the trunk door wide open for seeing the real Graves in a future movie. I hope he doesn't come face to face with Credence!

Gellert Grindelwald

Grindelwald is the character in this story who was most established in Harry Potter canon. However, we see very little of what can be called true Grindelwald in *Fantastic Beasts*. Whether Grindelwald had Polyjuiced Graves or used another magical method to impersonate the Auror, the end result is that he still had to remain true to Graves' character.

From canon established in Harry Potter, we know that Grindelwald was a brilliant young man who became obsessed with establishing wizard dominance over Muggles. At first, he drew Dumbledore into his plans…until Dumbledore realized how dark those plans were. In their final quarrel, Dumbledore's younger sister, Ariana, was killed. Grindelwald and Dumbledore met again in 1945 when Dumbledore overpowered him in a duel and won the Elder Wand from him.

Our first encounter with Grindelwald in *Fantastic Beasts* is opposite to Voldemort in *Philosopher's Stone*. When first we saw Voldemort, he was at his lowest point of power. We are meeting Grindelwald at his most powerful and rising.

Grindelwald will be defeated; what remains to be seen is how. At some point, Dumbledore will figure into the story. Many fans cannot wait to see the young Dumbledore and the younger Grindelwald as they interact.

One new element introduced in the film is the hint of Grindelwald possessing the Inner Eye, as Trelawney would say.

Graves speaks to Credence of a vision he had regarding the Obscurial. He saw the child close to Credence's mother.

If Grindelwald possesses the Sight, it must need some fine tuning. His vision showed him the location of the Obscurial, but not his true identity. Perhaps he needs to partner with a Demiguise.

Let's hope he does not. Imagine a dark wizard possessing a keen enough vision to know where all his enemies are at all times. Or to know where the most powerful weapons are that he needs to fulfill his vision of the Greater Good. Terrifying.

As for Grindelwald's name, fans have had a long time to search this one. Most theorize it is based on the name of a village in Switzerland, which could possibly link him to Heinrich Eberstadt. There is also the theory that it's based on the giant Grendel in *Beowulf*.

The Barebones

The Barebones are a put-together family of Mary Lou's choice, not birth (much like the Sayre-Boot-Steward family that founded Ilvermorny). All three Barebone children were adopted, seemingly to suit Mary Lou's purpose to serve as her little army to squash magic out of the world. Nothing is ever mentioned of Mr. Barebone.

However, through Pottermore, we are given the history of Bartholomew Barebone, a Scourer descendent (for more on Scourers, see the Worldbuilding chapter). Bartholomew was a No-Maj who was so committed to exposing witches and wizards that he seduced a young witch, Dorcus Twelvetrees, into revealing many of its secrets. Mary Lou has ancient wizarding heritage, which is why she believes in it with so much passion and hatred.

The surname I find very intriguing. Its Dictionary.com meaning of "the most essential components," or reduced to the bare minimum, gives a hint of the Puritanical frugality and simplicity of the family. Perhaps, also, a hint toward one of the essential themes of the story?

With the naming of the three children as Credence (Faith), Chastity, and Modesty, I feel that Rowling is pointing a subtle finger to one of the most powerful and beloved scripture verses of all time. The Love Chapter, First Corinthians 13. In it, St. Paul writes of the nature of love and the faith of a child becoming mature. If we look to the King James Version, he speaks of faith, hope, and charity, whereas modern translation use faith, hope, and *love*.

1 Corinthians 13

1 If I speak in the tongues of men or of angels, but do not have love, I am only a resounding gong or a clanging cymbal.

2 If I have the gift of prophecy and can fathom all mysteries and all knowledge, and if I have a faith that can move mountains, but do not have love, I am nothing.

3 If I give all I possess to the poor and give over my body to hardship that I may boast, but do not have love, I gain nothing.

4 Love is patient, love is kind. It does not envy, it does not boast, it is not proud.

5 It does not dishonor others, it is not self-seeking, it is not easily angered, it keeps no record of wrongs.

6 Love does not delight in evil but rejoices with the truth.

7 It always protects, always trusts, always hopes, always perseveres.

8 Love never fails. But where there are prophecies, they will cease; where there are tongues, they will be stilled; where there is knowledge, it will pass away.

9 For we know in part and we prophesy in part,

10 but when completeness comes, what is in part disappears.

11 When I was a child, I talked like a child, I thought like a child, I reasoned like a child. When I became a man, I put the ways of childhood behind me.

12 For now we see only a reflection as in a mirror; then we shall see face to face. Now I know in part; then I shall know fully, even as I am fully known.

13 And now these three remain: faith, hope and love. But the greatest of these is love. (New International Version)

In a verse that speaks to the power of love as the greatest power on earth, there are also hints of other themes Rowling works with: prophecy, tongues (speaking in foreign languages), faith, and hidden knowledge.

You can see why this verse would appeal to Rowling. If she is indeed drawing from it in naming her Barebone family, we must consider the purpose of her twists. First, Rowling is known for twisting her most important clues to make them harder to find. If she had named the three children Faith, Hope, and Love, that would have been too easy. She gives us Faith in the more masculinized and hidden version of Credence. Then she twists Charity into Chastity. So what of Hope to Modesty?

I would like to speculate here that Mary Lou, a modernized Puritan, may have changed the real names of the children when they were adopted. Though Chastity's name is closer linked to Charity and thus to Love, it is my guess that when we discover the birth name of Modesty, it will bear a stronger link to love. Speaking to Graves, Credence mentions how much his younger sister has missed her birth family, whom she obviously loved. It is to this home that she flees after her adopted family is destroyed.

There is another aspect to the Barebone surname that may also hint at where Rowling is going. Praise-God Barebone (truly that is his name!) was a 17th century English preacher best remembered for his participation in the Fifth Monarchists. What's so fascinating about these Fifth Monarchists in relation to Rowling's work, aside from the number five theme, is their apocalyptic belief system, which will be discussed more in the Themes chapter.

Finally, Rowling hints strongly that Credence's mother was a witch. And Modesty has a fascination with magic. Mary Lou seems to have "rescued" her children from magical homes to "squash the magic" out of them, as Vernon Dursley so strongly desired with Harry. Could each one of these children have an important role to play in the series?

Mary Lou Barebone

In her "1920s version of Puritan dress" (p. 10), Mary Lou Barebone is Rowling's most hated character come back to life—Dolores Umbridge. Just like Umbridge, Mary Lou is a nasty woman who manipulates and abuses children as a means to her own aims and ambitions. And just like Umbridge, she seems to delight in inflicting both emotional and physical wounds on those she is supposed to nurture and protect. In fact, the wounds she inflicts on Credence's hand, which Graves heals, is strongly reminiscent of Umbridge's "lines" with Harry.

In her passion to squash the magic out of the children she's adopted, Mary Lou is also strikingly similar to Vernon Dursley. However, Vernon only took in one child, and was forced to at that. Mary Lou has willingly adopted three.

In the makeup of the Barebone family, I see a twisted reflection to the founding family of Ilvermorny. However, Isolt and James adopted Chadwick and Webster and raised them with love. The founding of Ilvermorny was largely to educate their sons to fulfill their magical potential.

As Mary Lou is dead by the end of the first movie, I see her as a character designed to set up some of Rowling's most important themes. Her backstory as a descendant of Scourers brings this history of magical abuse and then separation into the contemporary times of *Fantastic Beasts*. Her church and organization under the name Second Salemers hints at the film's apocalyptic themes. And her personal abuse and neglect of the children in her care is a reflection of Rowling's own personal crusade to improve lives for all neglected children through her Lumos Foundation.[5]

Chastity Barebone

Chastity may not have much of a role to play in the plot of this story, nor going forward as she was killed when Credence attacked Mary Lou. But her position gives us some insight toward the Barebones and some of the themes Rowling is weaving into the series.

Chastity is described as an adult in Rowling's first mention in the script book. Of the three Barebone children, Chastity seems the one most obedient to Mary Lou. The children who come to them for meals look toward Chastity when grabbing their leaflets. She is described with words

---

[5] https://wearelumos.org/

like "primly" and "shy" and "formulaically."

The camera follows her POV twice: first, when walking through the church to open the door for the children to come in, and second when she's looking upward to where Mary Lou is about to whip Credence. But Rowling gives no hint of her expression. Like her very name, Chastity seems restrained in every way.

If Mary Lou was indeed forming her family from the children of witches and wizards, what then might we learn about Chastity going forward, even if she is truly dead?

Her one line is very suspicious:

Hand out your leaflets! I'll know if you dump 'em. Tell me if you see anything suspicious. (p. 154)

Is she just threatening the children to keep them from throwing the leaflets away? Or does she truly have the magical ability to see what they do with them?

Credence Barebone

Credence's section here will be brief as much of the aspects of his character are covered under other headings and chapters. His role as the Obscurial is discussed elsewhere.

Although the "faith" part of his name is mentioned above, there is another meaning for Credence that I believe pertains. In the Church's Eucharist (Mass), the credence is the table which holds the bread and wine before they are consecrated and served.

In this sense, Credence holds the elements that can be come Divine…if lovingly nurtured. With the power Credence possesses, he could be quite the force for good.

In the script book, he is described as an adult. In the film, he comes off as an older teen, at least to me.

All we know about his heritage before he was adopted by Mary Lou is that his mother was a "wicked, unnatural woman" (p. 204). A witch.

Based on his interactions with Graves, Credence longs for a connection to his magical heritage, which he has been taught to fear and loathe. Self-loathing is perhaps the most destructive form of hatred.

Graves/Grindelwald decreases Credence's self-worth even more when he betrays his blossoming romantic feelings by telling him:

You're a Squib, Credence. I could smell it off you the minute I met you. (p. 226).

He then tells Credence that the death of his mother is his reward. (We assume he is referring to Mary Lou and that Grindelwald has not searched out Credence's birth mother).

It's quite a bleak beginning for this young man. However, Rowling loves to take a dark character with a kernel of good and redeem them (Snape, anyone?). We must have faith in Credence.

Modesty Barebone

At eight, Modesty is the youngest of the adopted Barebone children. We have no idea how long ago she joined the family, but as Credence informs us, she still misses her eleven brothers and sisters. Perhaps this is why she, above the older Chastity and Credence, shows more spirit and rebels against Mary Lou. You have to cheer when she throws her Second Salemer leaflets into the air in glee, despite Chastity's warnings.

The biggest hint of something more going on with Modesty comes when Credence sneaks into her bedroom, believing her to be the Obscurial.

> A single bed, an oil lamp, a sampler on the wall: AN ALPHABET OF SIN. Modesty's dolls lined up on a shelf. One with a little noose around its neck, another tied to a stake.
>
> (p. 201).

It's a bleak room, witness to a bleak childhood. No wonder in her fantasies, magic would seem a wondrous gift rather than the abomination her Ma makes it to be. Perhaps that's why she hid away the toy wand Credence finds.

In the confrontation that follows, while we know it is Credence who kills Mary Lou as the Obscurus, it appears to be Modesty who snatches the belt out of her hands with magic. Modesty who makes the belt slither out of her reach like a snake. And Modesty who looks back at her mother with defiance.

For Modesty is the defiant one. Defiantly she sought to protect her older brother against the foul Senator. Afraid and upset when their mother beats him, Modesty showed love in protecting her older brother from the woman who was supposed to love and nurture him. If the hint of magic in Modesty is real, I believe she will play a key role in saving Credence before series end.

One last question regarding Modesty—where did she get the wand from? Was it really a toy, or was it given her as a nod of encouragement from an interested party?

I'll discuss the chant Modesty sings in the Plot chapter.

Seraphina Picquery

For me, Madam Seraphina Picquery is a more intelligent version of Fudge. She's very much a politician, but one who carries her responsibilities seriously.

In her name, Seraphina appears to be a reference to the seraphim, angels of the highest order, associated with white light and purity. For this story, that's not necessarily a good thing (see White and Blue in the Plot chapter for more). Interestingly, the term seraph was also used in the Hebrew Bible (Old Testament) to indicate a serpent, and Picquery was in the Horned Serpent House at Ilvermorny (via Pottermore).

As for the source for *Picquery*, a 1000-year-old book of magic and astrology intrigues me. Originally written in Arabic, *Picatrix* is a 400-page guide that brings together much of the understanding of esoteric thought and practices of its day. In what is considered by conventional standards to be a chaotic manner, it covered alchemy, astrology, and talismanic magic and the people who practiced them. The book warrants greater research and reflection, and I hope to cover more of it at my BeastChaser.com blog. Join me!

In personality, Madam Picquery comes across as a strong woman determined to do her job of protecting the secrecy and thus safety of the wizarding world. Her most troublesome aspect for me was not her low treatment of Tina, though that did make me question her nature, but her lack of hesitation in ordering the killing of Credence. In this, she shows an almost cruel inflexibility in upholding the law that is only alleviated slightly when she allows the Team to say goodbye to Jacob at the end. Whether a strict adherence to law is morally justified over a more compassionate approach is a question I expect to see explored more fully as we go forward.

In an interesting exchange on Twitter shortly after the film released, Rowling hinted at the dark ambiguity between right and wrong that Picquery and Grindelwald both aroused:

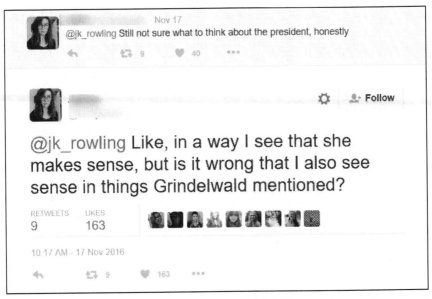

Questions of right vs wrong and rigidity in beliefs often point to a dualistic way of thinking that may be challenged in this series. (For a hint of this, see the discussion of *Khora* under Occamy in the Beast chapter.) Whether Madam Picquery will carry forward in future movies remains to be seen. But it's for sure that the moral and ethical questions her character raises will continue to form conflict within the story.

Henry Shaw, Sr.

Henry Shaw, Sr. is a man who exudes power. Described in the text as a "newspaper magnate" (p. 71), Shaw rules over his media empire from his penthouse apartment in a tower named after himself (perhaps hinting at Trump), conversing with his favored son whom he's grooming and promoting for the presidency, with a commanding view of the city he holds power over.

Shaw's belief that no one "gives away anything valuable for free" (p. 73) tells us more about himself than it does about Mary Lou. Though he does not possess the nasty edge of his Senator son, he's also shown to be brusque with his younger son and terse to the point of rude with the Barebones.

From his appearance at the City Hall subway when the Obscurus is trapped, we see a father intent on revenge, threatening to expose those responsible. And he's not easily frightened, remaining as others flee, to not only watch what transpires with the Obscurus, but to direct his photographers to take pictures.

What do you think? Would those old black and white negatives survive a memory charm? Even a very wet one?

As for his name, it's my suspicion that Shaw's name is derived from George Bernard Shaw. It is the author's various political stances and beliefs that make me feel he served as Rowling's inspiration. As a vocal member of the early Fabian Society, Shaw wrote numerous pamphlets promoting their social reform policies, which included eugenics (at that time).

But it is his later positioning with fascist world leaders which I think links him best with Henry Shaw:

A *New York Times* report dated 10 December 1933 quoted a recent Fabian Society lecture in which Shaw had praised Hitler, Mussolini and Stalin: "[T]hey are trying to get something done, [and] are adopting methods by which it is possible to get something done." (Wikipedia.org)

With his talk with Junior of buying "the boats" (p. 71), Henry Shaw shows a willingness to adopt any method to obtain his goals, and will not easily forgive the loss of his favored son and their dreams of power. Should Shaw Sr. appear again in future movies, and should his photos have survived the Swooping Evil memory charm, then his personal devastation will not bode well for the magical world.

Senator Henry Shaw

Senator Shaw is the favored son of his father. He appears the confident, polished politician with the nasty private side. The way he treats Credence, a young man he just met, is horrible.

Also, the conversation that is interrupted when Langdon enters his father's office with the Barebones sounds very suspicious:

Senator Shaw

...we could just buy the boats... (p. 71).

"Boats" sounds an awful lot like "votes." But even if not, I doubt his desire to buy the boats is charitable.

The Senator shows no affection for his younger brother, and the way he looks at Credence and then attacks him verbally, calling him a freak and saying they all belong in the trash, shows a man who preys on the weak.

At the high-society dinner in his honor, we're told he has aspirations of the presidency. He acts the ultimate politician, bounding on the stage, pointing and winking at people in the crowd then makes campaign pledges to banish pool halls and private parlors.

When the "beast" that kills him rips at his poster, we know it is not an accidental death. As he seems to be truly dead, I doubt he will contribute much to the series going forward. The effect he had on Credence, however, will.

Langdon Shaw

Rowling goes to great lengths to describe Langdon as the less favored son and to show that he is disrespected by both his family and the people who work for them. When he brings the Barebones to his father's newspaper office, the way the others react show that it's not the first time he's gone off on something they consider "harebrained." Meanwhile, Langdon is doing his best to look important to the Barebones.

Later, at his brother's death, Rowling describes Langdon as "determined, perhaps triumphant," as he cries: "Witches!" (p. 140).

His father seems to value Langdon more after his brother's death. Standing by his father's side in the subway during the Obscurus scene, he appears enthralled with the power of the magic.

Langdon is a character who was fascinated with magic before he witnessed it, then completely captivated upon observing its power. He was shown twice at his father's side following the favored son's death. Should these characters carry forward into the series, I imagine that the powerful Shaw Sr. will be more open, even with their memories wiped, to believe his son's magical fascination and use it to seek revenge.

I admit to being stumped as to where the name Langdon comes from, if it has any special meaning. Langdon is a common place name in the UK, and as Rowling has a fondness for place names, this may be all it is.

One other possibility intrigues me, however. Robert Langdon was the main character from Dan Brown's bestselling *The DaVinci Code* and other books in that series. The link I see here is that Brown's character studied religious symbols to figure out clues to a criminal and historical puzzle, much as we are doing with Rowling's script.

Barker

Henry Shaw, Sr.'s assistant. His main action in the story is his intent on keeping Langdon away from his father. Later, he arrives with Shaw Sr. as he approaches the subway where the Obscurus is contained.

Regarding his name—the most interesting Barker I found was Benjamin Barker, the name of Sweeney Todd in the 1979 musical adaptation of *Sweeney Todd: The Demon Barber of Fleet Street*.

I hope Langdon doesn't need any haircuts.

Mr. Bingley

The most intriguing aspect about Bingley at this point is his name, and the fact that he is important enough to name. If he is a link to the Mr. Bingley of *Pride and Prejudice* knowing Rowling is a huge Austen fan, what does his name signify? Is it a nod to Austen's well-loved character, or to a theme of her novel?

One possible link I see between *Fantastic Beasts* and *Pride and Prejudice* is the development of two parallel love stories: Newt with Tina and Queenie with Jacob. As the secondary pair, could Jacob's meeting with Mr. Bingley be a tip of the hat to the link between Austen's and Rowling's characters? Jacob is a good-hearted fellow, like Bingley, and Queenie is "…the most beautiful girl ever to don witches' robes" (p. 79). Jane is considered a great beauty, her mother remarking, "I was sure you could not be so beautiful for nothing!" Indeed, when Jacob says "Mr. Bingley!" in the vault scene, you can almost hear Mrs. Bennett's shrill cry. (For more on this thread, see the chapter on Shipping.)

Other notes worth mentioning…in the script, the bank is referred to as Bingley's Bank, though that may not be its formal title. And near the end of the book, Bingley is referred to as "the bank manager" (p. 262).

Finally, as if to make sure we noticed Mr. Bingley and remember him going forward, he appears at the end among the No-Maj having their memories washed clean. Mr. Bingley is in his shower, his wife nearby brushing her teeth.

Abernathy

Abernathy is a MACUSA employee and Tina's boss. Rowling describes him as a "pompous jobsworth," which, for us non-Brits, characterizes "inflexible employees, petty rule-following and excessive administration."[6]

While he is rude to Tina, he seems to have a thing for Queenie. When he stops Queenie during the MACUSA escape scene, he is shown "straightening his tie, trying to appear calm and authoritative— Queenie obviously makes him nervous." (p. 177). At the end, she leaves him with his heart racing.

As I'm already shipping Jakweenie[7], I'm hoping Abernathy doesn't rock the boat!

Leta Lestrange

Leta does not appear onscreen in this first movie. Only her beautiful picture does, carefully kept inside Newt's case. However, as it has already been revealed that she will have an onscreen role in the next movie, she warrants an in-depth study.

Leta is an old, "real close" friend of Newt's from Hogwarts. By benefit of Queenie's Legilimency, we know that their relationship left Newt hurting and that Leta was a "taker."

One of Leta's descendants by marriage is surely Bellatrix Lestrange. The family's reputation of dark magic and Pureblood mania must be well established even in this generation as even Queenie, all the way in America, seems to have heard of them: "Aren't they kinda—you know" (p. 218).

The only other clue about Leta is from Newt:

...neither of us really fitted in at school (p. 219).

Newt and Leta bonded as outsiders, kind of like Albus Potter and Scorpius Malfoy, almost an exact century later. (Hmm, wonder if there will be more overlaps from *Cursed Child?*)

As for Leta's name, Leda was the queen of Sparta and mother of Helen of Troy. Helen was born of her union with Zeus, who came to her in the form of a swan. This link to the Trojan War and the *Iliad* is covered in the Myth chapter.

---

[6] https://en.wikipedia.org/wiki/Jobsworth
[7] Rowling Tweeted this ship name on November 24, 2016.

In considering the source of Leta's name, I would also like to note an early 20th century American psychologist by the name Leta Stetter Hollingworth. She is remembered for her pioneering research of gifted children as she advocated for their differentiation in the educational system to better meet their needs and prepare them to contribute to society.

What intrigues me most about Hollingworth in regard to Leta Lestrange is that Rowling's Leta, like Newt, shared a similar interest in unusual beasts. With a story that focuses on exceptional children in the form of the Obscurials, perhaps we may see her interest switch to the beastly parasites that affect these children when she appears in the next movie.

While I don't think Rowling would do another Lestrange/Chief Antagonist paring, it does seems more than coincidental that she's linked both Leta and Grindelwald with an interest in magical beasts that endanger other people's lives.

Dumbledore and His Family

I've included a section on Dumbledore and his family not because they play a role in this first movie, but because we know they will in those still to come.

We only get a hint of the backstory we already know between Dumbledore and Grindelwald in the scene of Newt's arrest at MACUSA:

Graves

...Yet one of your teachers argued strongly against your expulsion. Now, what makes Albus Dumbledore so fond of you? (p. 157)

That Dumbledore's name raised a question from Graves was one important clue as to his secret identity. Yet this was Dumbledore's only mention, aside from a flashed news article in the magazine *Transfiguration Today* written by him below another post on animagi. This raises an old favorite fan question—was Dumbledore, a transfiguration teacher, also an animagi?

For now, in *Fantastic Beasts* there were other hints to remind us of Dumbledore and the backstory of his family. Graves' first name, Percival, is one of Dumbledore's middle names (Albus Percival Wulfric Brian Dumbledore). I do not think that a coincidence. Was Rowling merely hinting at a link between the two men? Or, was she perhaps hinting that

Grindelwald took on this Percival's identity because it made him feel closer to his old lover?

When the International Confederation of Wizards descends on MACUSA, we should remember one important piece of Potter history—at some point in time, Dumbledore served as their Supreme Mugwump. I would guess that we will see him in this role before series end.

But there is an even more important allusion to Dumbledore's family—the Obscurus. Many fans have already connected the dots between what Fantastic Beasts shows us about Obscurials and how Dumbledore's younger sister was described with magic exploding out of her because of the severe trauma she had experienced as a child.

Whether Ariana will turn out to be an Obscurial or not, Dumbledore and his family are sure to make a significant appearance throughout the series...and we'll be watching!

Theseus Scamander, Newt's Older brother

Theseus has a sole reference in the movie during the International Confederation of Wizards meeting, where he is mentioned as a war hero. I'm assuming that's World War I.

As for his name—There are a number of myths associated with Theseus, a mythical king of Athens, including his slaying of the Minotaur and his six labors through the Underworld. This myth link will bear watching as we also have an Ariadne in the Dumbledore's sister, Ariana. Ariadne is a version of Ariana. Will Theseus follow a thread linking these two stories?

However, coupled with the last name Scamander, the myth that interests me the most is his connection with Troy. Theseus abducted Helen (later, of Troy) in her youth. Her other suitors rescued her and pledged to come to her assistance in the future should she be abducted again. This pact is what led to the great war against Troy when she was abducted by Prince Paris.

In fact, Theseus was quite the lady's man, with associations not only with Helen and Ariadne, but with Hippolyta and Phaedra.

Is it possible that Newt lives in his brother's shadow, much as Ron did with his brothers as well as Harry?

Mrs. Esposito

Mrs. Esposito is briefly heard onscreen as Tina's landlady. Although she does not appear on stage, we hear only her voice offstage asking if Tina is alone when she sneaks in with Newt and Jacob, her name is intriguing.

Esposito is an Italian surname that means "exposed," often used for foundling babies.

Who has been exposed? Is it Tina and Queenie, living in this house? Or will the landlady one day be exposed as a magical being watching over the orphaned Goldstein sisters like Mrs. Figg did for Harry all those years in the future?

Heinrich Eberstadt

Eberstadt is the first man speaking when we enter the International Confederacy of Wizards scene in the Pentagram Office. He is described in the script book as being a Swiss delegate.

Heinrich is a German name that means ruler of the home[8].

One of the most infamous Heinrichs in history is Heinrich Himmler, a Nazi SS commander who oversaw the building of the concentration camps and directed the killings. See the Forecast chapter for more on this topic.

There is also a possible link to Heinrich Schliemann, an amateur German archaeologist who discovered the remains of Troy in Turkey. For more on this, see the Myth chapter.

Darmstadt-Eberstadt in Germany is home to the Frankenstein castle. The possible allusion to Mary Shelley's scientist who created the monster is intriguing. See the Obscurus section in the Myth chapter for more on this.

Besides his name, Rowling throws out two other clues about him:
1) He is a delegate from Switzerland (see International Confederation of Wizards in Worldbuilding for more).
2) According to Madam Picquery, he let Grindelwald slip through his fingers.

One has to wonder, was this last truly a slip, or deliberate?

All of these hints suggest that we will be seeing this character again in future books and that he has a crucial role to play.

Momolu Wotorson

Momolu Wotorson is mentioned once in the script as a the delegate in the International Confederation of Wizards scene. He's the one who

---

[8] http://www.babynames.com/name/Heinrich

mistakes Newt for his brother Theseus, the war hero.

Momolu is a popular surname in Liberia, and TLC Africa lists it as a Muslim boy's name.[9] One well-known person of this name was Momulu Massaquoi, a Liberian diplomat in German from 1922-1930.

Wotorson is also a surname from Liberia and Kenya. From these two name hints, I would guess this character is from Liberia. Liberia entered WWII in 1944 on the side of the Allies, although the country had been supporting the United States prior to its entry by providing rubber.

The fact that this character is named leads me to believe we may see him again, and that he is another strong hint that the series may go into Africa at some point. For more, see International Confederation of Wizards under Worldbuilding, and Five Locations in Theme.

Gnarlak

An informant of Tina's when she was an Auror, Gnarlak is a Mafia-boss goblin at the Blind Pig who has been known to buy and sale magical creatures. His dress and demeanor give him a slick and sly look.

> **Gnarlak sits himself at the end of their table, an air of confidence and dangerous control. A house-elf hastily brings him a drink. (p. 194)**

Totally in control of everything and everyone around him, he has information, of course, but it won't come cheaply. However, the only thing Newt has to offer that interests him is a frozen Ashwinder egg. Then Gnarlak spots Pickett and determines he must have the Bowtruckle's ability to pick locks for himself.

The scene of Newt handing over Pickett, the little Bowtruckle pleading and clinging to his fingers, is heartbreaking.

Gnarlak also shows the extension of his underground connections in his response to Newt's question, hinting that he knows about Graves:

> *You ask too many questions, Mr. Scamander. That can get you killed. (p. 198)*

As for Gnarlak's name, I'm guessed it comes from *gnarled* as his fingers are all twisted and gnarly in the movie.

If Gnarlak didn't get arrested because of being knocked out cold when

---

[9] http://www.tlcafrica.com/african_names.htm

the Aurors arrive, thanks to Jacob, we may see him again. I'm worried that he may seek to reclaim Pickett.

Looking Forward

One of the biggest questions I have going forward into the next movie relates to the new location. It's already been announced that the second movie will be based in Paris. As such, I would not expect the full cast of New York characters to ship overseas. While I analyzed each character with the possibility of a future appearance, my guess is that we'll see the main characters and perhaps a couple of the others. Then we'll be treated to a new set of French characters! Fingers crossed that we'll meet at least one of Fleur's ancestors.

I've read a couple of reports that Newt will not remain the main character as the movies move forward, that the attention will shift to Grindelwald and Dumbledore. However, Rowling recently Tweeted this reassurance for Newt fans:

J.K. Rowling @jk_rowling · Nov 24
Of course.

@jk_rowling please tell us newt is still main character in the next movies

4.1K   9.9K

Secret Four

Pickett Picks the Lock

(The Plot and its Clues)

Two of the key mysteries throughout the Harry Potter series were:

1) Would Harry live or die by series end? and
2) Where was the brewing war between Voldemort and the wizarding world headed?

In Fantastic Beasts, Rowling has a tougher job ahead as we already know the answer to these two questions:

1) According to canon, Newt Scamander lives to a ripe old age. He was at one point detected on the Marauder's Map in Harry's third year.
2) We know from the time period and information given in interviews that Fantastic Beasts will be entering WWII. What we don't know is how the Wizarding World, or our characters, will interact with it.

For Rowling, to create a compelling mystery where the ultimate fate of the main hero and the world are not as in question will prove a greater challenge. In the first movie, we have the plot and a subplot. While Newt's plot is fairly simple—to find and protect his beasts, it's the hidden nature of the secondary plot that drives the story forward.

This plot is driven by Grindelwald in disguise. He is the one trying to find and control the child with a curse attached. It is his search, and Credence's reaction to it, which primarily drives the story forward. Newt Scamander's release of the creatures into this same society complicates Grindelwald's search and is where the two plots intersect.

In this chapter, we will first examine the plot, especially as it relates to the Newt's Hero's Journey. Then we'll follow the trail of clues Rowling weaves throughout this current plot to guess at what is to come.

The Monomyth, aka The Hero's Journey

For plot, we turn to the oldest plot structure remembered. Many of you will already be familiar with the theories of comparative mythologist Joseph Campbell. His seminal work, *A Hero with a Thousand Faces*, presented the idea of the monomyth, also known as the Hero's Journey. Or you might be more familiar with the book *The Writer's Journey* by story consultant and screenwriter Christopher Vogler. Vogler studied Campbell's work and presented the mythologist's complex theories in a condensed and more accessible form for writers.

Campbell's comparative studies of hundreds of myths showed striking commonalities among stories separated by centuries, cultures, and continents. Like Jung, he theorized that these points of congruence thrive due to archetypal knowledge and understanding, which exists in all peoples, and that bridges separation of time and space. Thus, the monomyth is a universal pattern of story structure that transcends human boundaries. It bubbles up in myths from ancient Greece, to medieval courtly romances, to today's commercial fiction. To put it simply—the Hero's Journey is the story plot which has lasted the longest because it strikes a universal human chord of truth.

As such the Hero's Journey is the archetypal outline for a blockbuster plot. Since the 1940s when its modern face was reinterpreted by Campbell in *A Hero with a Thousand Faces*, many books and movies have been based on it, most famously the *Star Wars* series by George Lucas.

The summaries of the steps of the Hero's Journey provided below are based on Vogler's presentation of Campbell's work. I'm going with Vogler because he simplifies the steps, which makes it a bit easier to understand. Please note that Vogler wrote a whole book on this journey, and we're covering it in a few pages. Thus I'll not discuss all the variations and nuances of style the Hero's Journey affords. I highly recommend you read Vogler, or if you love mythology and esoteric studies as I do, try Campbell.

Also, I'm adding a thread at the beginning that is not part of Vogler's twelve-step Hero's Journey, even though he discusses it. **Theme, or the Central Question of the Work,** is to me the hub of the wheel around which all elements of the story revolve, including the plot. Each step of the

Hero's Journey will pull from and flow back into the theme or the central question. You'll see it clearly in my analysis of Rowling's work and could be viewed as the impetus for the beginning of the Hero's Journey and in the character fulfillment at the end, coming full circle.

Vogler's Twelve Steps to the Hero's Journey in Fantastic Beasts

First, we'll look at brief summaries of each of the twelve steps of the Hero's Journey. Then, I'll share a table summarizing how it is presented within Fantastic Beasts. Finally, we'll break the table summary down into more detailed analysis of how Rowling implements each of the steps.

For easier reading, there is a pdf version available at the publisher's website www.DeepRiver.press on the Fantastic Beast page. The chart is coded with *italics*, **bold print,** and ALL CAPS is to help your eye follow similar items across the seven columns of the table.

Note: These steps do not always happen sequentially. Rowling tends to have the Resurrection before the Road Back.

Twelve Steps of the Hero's Journey

(modified from Christopher Vogler's *The Writer's Journey*)

Ordinary World—The home base of the hero, his normal everyday world. The Ordinary World should be in sharp contrast to the world he's getting ready to venture into, the Special World. Usually, the problem the hero will face already exists in his Ordinary World, but lies dormant.

Call to Adventure—A discovery or arrival that hints at a new world and calls the heroine within, a challenge or wrong done that must be answered. The Call to Adventure prompts the heroine to leave her Ordinary World for the Special World. It could be something that threatens the peace of the Ordinary World if the heroine does not go off to deal with it.

Refusal of the Call—The moment in which the hero hesitates, not sure whether he wants to change. By refusing the Call, the hero shows that he fully understands the serious nature of the Adventure, that his life will be threatened or seriously altered. Does he want to take that risk, or stay safe with the status quo? Can he truly make a difference?

Meeting with the Mentor and Gift—The mentor serves as the guide for the Hero's Journey. He's the old wise wizard who trains and tests the hero, and gives gifts to enable the completion of the hero's quest (not do it for him).

Crossing the First Threshold—The portal from the Ordinary World to the Special World, usually guarded by a Guardian or Gatekeeper. It is symbolic of the heroine having made a firm commitment by taking that first major step to begin her quest. Gatekeepers serve to test whether the heroine is worthy to pass.

Tests, Allies, Enemies—This is where the hero is prepared for the Ordeal to come by developing skills and facing tests, meeting and accepting allies, and learns who his enemies are. A hero cannot simply enter the Special World and triumph. There would be no growth arc. He must be challenged, learn, and grow in order to succeed. This is where you get to truly torture your hero!

Approach to the Inmost Cave—As the heroine approaches the Inmost Cave, the place of her greatest challenge, she will face new and more difficult obstacles and guardians to overcome to prove herself worthy for that ultimate battle. The Inmost Cave represents the classic Underworld, and the heroine must be prepared to journey through it, face death, and be reborn. Often, the heroine may pause, tempted to turn back, knowing the horrors she's about to face.

The Ordeal—In the Inmost Cave the heroine must face her deepest fears. Using all the skills she's learned up to now, she confronts the antagonist/villain and faces the ultimate test, the culmination of the trials that have prepared her for this final battle. Here she faces either literal or symbolic death. She must face some form of death in order to experience resurrection.

Reward (Seizing the Sword)—The reward is something the hero wins or steals from the Ordeal that is a trophy of sorts, marking his triumph over the antagonist. The Reward is personal, and most powerful as a symbol of the book's theme or central question. It may not always be material, but could be presented as a celebration or a love scene.

The Road Back—The bridge from the Special World to the Ordinary World. Here the hero crosses another threshold that may include a reassessment and rededication of goals. The Hero must decide whether to return to the Ordinary World rather than to remain in the Special World. Oftentimes, the hero may be chased out of the Special World by those he opposed, or may find the defeated Villain rallying for a second round.

Resurrection—That moment when either literally or symbolically the heroine is reborn. This may be brought about by a rebounding villain who must be conquered once more. The heroine awakens to a new world and a transformed life. Generally speaking, it happens on the Road Back because a bit of reflection is usually necessary to understand the transformation that occurred as a result of the Ordeal. It conveys the idea of cleansing, of baptism. The stench of the Ordeal, of death, must be washed away for the heroine to reenter the community.

Return with the Elixir—The Elixir is like the reward except it benefits someone beyond the hero. Sometimes the two may be combined, but the Elixir is usually a gift that has the power to heal the hero's wounded community. It can also heal or benefit an individual. The important aspect is that it is something the hero has gained from the Special World that benefits others beyond himself (whereas the Reward after the Ordeal benefited the hero, or was a trophy of the hero's triumph).

The Hero's Journey in Fantastic Beasts

Guiding Theme; Central Desire or Question	Protecting the powerless vs. the Greater Good Above all else, Newt seeks to protect and preserve his magical creatures.
Step 1 Ordinary World	The montage of newspapers show the Ordinary World, even though it is under extraordinary circumstances. Also, the brief scene of Newt on the ship talking to his animals.
Step 2 Call to Adventure	Mary Lou's call out to Newt. Niffler escapes.
Step 3 Refusal of the Call	Newt responds to Mary Lou that he's more of a Chaser. Trying to recapture the Niffler.
Step 4 Meeting with the Mentor Gift	**Mentor**: Tina—She is the one that knows this Special World and introduces him to it. **Her gift**: Introduces him to Graves/Grindelwald, which may relate to his secret mission. (See Plot chapter).
Step 5 Crossing the First Threshold; Guardian	Entering MACUSA For Newt, unlike Harry, his special world is not the new world of magic. His special world is New York City.

Step 6 Tests; Allies; ENEMIES	**Tests**: recovering beasts, surviving death chamber, The Blind Pig **Allies**: Tina, Jacob, Queenie **Enemies**: Graves/Grindelwald, Gnarlak, Madam Picquery I include Picquery because she was an antagonist, and possibly villain.
Step 7 Approach to the Inmost Cave	Approach to the subway, race across rooftops Inmost Cave: Subway
Step 8 Ordeal: Opponent faced; Triumph over opponent; **Death experience** (may be symbolic)	**Ordeal**: Saving the Obscurus, facing Graves/Grindelwald **Opponent**: Grindelwald **Faces death** in Graves/Grindelwald's attack. Saved by Credence turning back into the Obscurus. **Triumph**: Captures Grindelwald, Tina seizes his wand.
Step 9 Reward (Seizing the Sword)	Grindelwald's wand, together with Tina.
Step 10 The Road Back	New York being repaired and goodbye scene with Jacob?
Step 11 Resurrection	Frank's loving embrace of Newt and then the storm scene. (See Baptism in Theme for more).
Step 12 Return with the Elixir	Grindelwald is captured (though we don't know for how long). New York's No-Maj world has been restored, and the protective divide of its magical world replaced.

There seems to be a bit of miscommunication between Rowling and her director as to who is going to be the chief protagonist going forward. David Yates indicated in an interview that he thought the story would shift more to Grindelwald and Dumbledore. But Rowling said on Twitter that

Newt would remain lead.[10]

Therefore, I think we can expect to see the continued focus on protecting the animals and a possible revelation regarding Newt's hidden mission, if there is one.

Rowling's Sleight of Hand

In weaving the mystery through her world of magic and myth, Rowling is the master magician. Her technique focuses heavily on that old reliable magician's trick: sleight of hand.

> Misdirection is perhaps the most important component of the art of sleight of hand. Using misdirection, the skillful magician choreographs every movement in a routine so even the most critical and observant spectators are *compelled to look where the magician wants them to*.
>
> (https://en.wikipedia.org/wiki/Sleight_of_hand)

Rowling lays some clues close to the surface which she intends for the reader to find easily. Then there are others where she uses sleight of hand to misdirect her fans, while still playing fair by having laid it.

While hiding her most important clues, Rowling uses her strongest clues to divert her readers elsewhere. In the clues we'll examine below, these are the specific techniques she's used to mark or hide them, depending on her intention to draw the reader's attention, or distract them from it.

1) Divert with action.

2) Distract with high emotions.

3) Give meaningful names (as discussed in the Character chapter).

4) Camouflage by use of myths and folklore.

5) Mark with repeated clues.

6) Reverse expectations.

7) Juxtapose the villain with the scene of the crime.

---

[10] https://twitter.com/jk_rowling/status/801727605951123456

The New York Ghost

The New York wizarding newspaper is probably a play on The New York Post. I see two hints with Rowling choosing *ghost* for the paper:

1) Ghosts rise from the grave. It's another running bit hinting at Graves as being suspicious.
2) As the American wizarding community is more separated from the No-Maj than the British, their world is even more underground.

Newt's Objective

Newt says initially that he came to NY to purchase an Appaloosa Puffskein as a gift, the only breeder living in NY. But Tina informs him:

...we closed that guy down a year ago. We don't allow the breeding of magical creatures in New York. (p. 38)

Wouldn't Newt, in his profession, be aware of this? Still, he seems to acknowledge that the Puffskein was just a cover when he informs Jacob that his real reason in coming was to release Frank, the Thunderbird, back into his home environment of Arizona.

There are other clues, however, that hint that even *this* excuse may still be a ruse. When Newt opens his case for the Customs inspector, a magnifying glass is partially covering a folded map. Its round glass magnifies the lettering "New York City Map" (clearly visible in a movie still).

Then, when we first see Newt walking the streets of New York, he is clutching "directions on a small piece of paper" (p. 9).

Directions? To where? And from whom?

And when Tina is hauling him into MACUSA, Newt objects:

Er— sorry, but I do have things to do, actually. (p. 36)

What does he have to do in New York? He gives every appearance of having a specific purpose, a mission. Not merely sightseeing.

Because of the link revealed later in the film of Newt to Dumbledore, and Graves'/Grindelwald's interest in Newt's connection to Dumbledore, many fans are speculating that Dumbledore could have sent Newt on a mission. And considering their past relationship as revealed in *Deathly Hallows*, Dumbledore could be tracking Grindelwald.

Is Newt's true purpose for coming to NY to find Grindelwald? And if so, knowing how manipulative and secretive Dumbledore can be, how aware is even Newt of his primary objective?

Threat-Level Clock

It's a huge Easter Egg for the reader when we see the Threat Level clock at MACUSA similar in purpose and type to the one Mrs. Weasley had to track the safety of her family members.

This clock, however, tracks the "Magical Exposure Threat Level" (p. 39) of the American wizarding community.

The first time it is seen, with the Obscurus causing damage but no deaths, the dial reads: "Severe Unexplained Activity."

After the death of Senator Shaw, however, when Tina runs past it to the meeting of the international wizards, it reads: Emergency

This clock hints at the separation of the No-Maj and Wizard world and how close they are to colliding.

Modesty's Hopscotch Chant

In a couple of different scenes in the Second Salem Church, we see Modesty skipping through chalked blocks, singing:

My momma, your momma,
gonna catch a witch,
My momma, your momma,
flying on a switch,
My momma, your momma,
witches never cry,
My momma, your momma,
witches gonna die! (p. 52)

Take out the repetitive "my momma, your momma," a hint as to who the witch is, and we have:

gonna catch a witch,
flying on a switch,
witches never cry,
witches gonna die!

Question—Why is the witch flying on a switch instead of the classical broom? Of course, a broom is a type of thick switch, but there are two other possible connotations I see here. One, is that the line's a play on a riding switch, another word for a horse crop. But more likely, Rowling is hinting at the switch used by parents to spank children.

And who is the *momma* we see spanking a child in *Fantastic Beasts?* Mary

Lou's preferred weapon, however, is Credence's own belt. She was also dead before the end of the film.

Mary Lou was a witch in both mannerisms and heredity. As the descendant of Scourers (see her character entry), she had a witch or wizard in her family tree. Through her myopic view of people different from herself and her mistreatment of the children who should be under her love and protection, she is presented as a cruel, abusive woman, hearkening back to an older understanding of *witch*.

So, Mary Lou, flying on her switch of a belt, never cried in her abusive treatment of Credence and died at the end of *Fantastic Beasts*.

As Modesty's chant continues with details of these witches' deaths:

> **Witch number one, drown in**
> **a river!**
> **Witch number two, gotta**
> **noose to give her!**
> **Witch number three . . . (p. 154)**

Notice that in page numbers, the above section with witch one and two comes after the stanza below with witch three and four. Rowling mixed it up a bit for us, not wanting to make it too easy. And perhaps to end on the most important one, for this book at least.

> **. . . Witch number three,**
> **gonna watch her burn,**
> **Witch number four, flogging**
> **take a turn. (p. 54)**

Drowning, hanging, burning, and flogging—while all are traditional methods for killing witches, my guess is that Rowling uses Modesty's chant to hint at particular deaths to come. Before series end, we can expect to see someone die from a variation on each of these, and we've already seen one.

While none of the three deaths in this first movie was a literal flogging, two were symbolically so. A flogging is a beating with a stick or whip. Senator Shaw and Mary Lou took a flogging by Obscurus, and Chastity was the casualty of this last attack. Shaw's scarred and broken body, which Mary Lou's later reflected, showed all evidence of having taken a beating.

I want you to notice something else about the four types of deaths mentioned. Something *elemental*:

1) "drown in a river" = **Water**
2) "gotta noose to give her" = suffocation, lack of **Air**
3) "gonna watch her burn" = **Fire**
4) "flogging take a turn" = a switch, from a tree, **Earth**

This elemental running bit will be found and highlighted a few times in this guide. The four elements run through the symbols of Ilvermorny and make up four parts of the theme of five, which this series is based on (see Myth chapter). Where is the fifth?

I'm willing to bet we'll here more of Modesty's chant in the second film to give us a hint of the most important "death."

White and Blue

Rowling has played with assigning meaning to colors before. Throughout Harry Potter, green was the color of Lily's eyes and *Avada Kedavra*. Pink was the color of concealment. And black, white, and red were levels of alchemy and symbols of Harry's progress to the gold of the Philosopher's Stone. (For more on the colors of alchemy, see *A Writer's Guide to Harry Potter*, which also references a fabulous essay, "Pink Stinks" by Julie Maffei, age 13).

To see what Rowling is hiding in this new series, I've listed every reference to the two most prominent colors mentioned below. For *Fantastic Beasts*, white is the new green.

All Things White:

1) A spell of "pure white light" which Grindelwald casts at five Aurors at the beginning of the film, killing them all.
2) The shining eyes of the Obscurus, visible from within his storm.
3) The executioners in MACUSA wear white coats.
4) The death chamber is a "pure white cell."
5) The spells in "electric blue and white" (p. 238-9) which the Aurors fire at the Obscurus as they chase him through the city.
6) When the Obscurus finally implodes, he becomes "a white ball of magical light taking over from the black mass" (p. 253).
7) The "wall of white light" (p. 255) that blocks Grindelwald from the Aurors and Newt and Tina. A forcefield of protection...or death.

All Things Blue:

1) Newt's overcoat, of course. Which he wears almost throughout the movie.
2) The Occamy.
3) The Billywig.
4) Tina's pajamas are blue, mentioned in the script.
5) Dougal the Demiguise's eyes when he's having a premonition.
6) Those spells, mentioned above, in "electric blue and white" (p. 238-9), shot at the Obscurus by the Aurors.
7) When Frank the Thunderbird flies through the storm carrying the vile of Swooping Evil venom, "The darkening sky flashes a brilliant blue and rain begins to fall" (p. 261).

While white is the color of killing or death, blue seems to be associated with life and hope. As such, it makes me wonder—of the spells shot by the Aurors at Credence as the Obscurus, perhaps not everyone was shooting to kill.

Squire's

The rooftop on which Newt and Team land to observe the Obscurus at full strength after Credence's betrayal by Graves is dominated by a large Squire's sign. This sign is specifically mentioned in the script book. As such, I suspect it has some meaning, but have not yet been able to pinpoint anything special.

I have two possibilities:

1) Most likely, it's meant to mark the New York City Squire, a hotel located near Times Square.
2) As for its deeper meaning, perhaps it's a nod to the Squire's Tale, an unfinished story within Chaucer's *Canterbury Tales*. If so, the magical gifts given to Genghis Kahn as part of the Squire's interrupted story would be most interesting to follow.
   a. A horse that teleports.
   b. A mirror that reads minds.
   c. A sword which is the only way to heal the wounds it creates.
   d. And a ring that allows the wearer to understand the language of birds.

Of these, Rowling has already used the ability to Apparate. Queenie is a Legilimens. Newt seems to understand all his beasts. Maybe we're on the lookout for another magical sword.

If you have ideas to share on this subject, please post them on my BeastChaser.com blog!

Animagi

I fully expect that an Animagi in hiding will appear within the series at some point. With that in mind, I watched carefully for any stray animal sightings within the script book. The one that intrigues me the most is the pigeon at the Second Salem Church that Credence scares away in scene 28. In fact, this scene, as written, is only two paragraphs long, and the first and longest of the two is all about the pigeon. It's as if this scene exists to show that pigeon.

Is the pigeon a witch or wizard watching over Credence?

The person I would most suspect of watching over him would be Teenie Tina. Maybe she can be very teeny, like a bird. And as it so happens, she has a magazine called *Transfiguration Today* in her apartment. If Tina were an Animagi, with her peaceful and somewhat awkward demeanor, I think a pigeon would suit her quite well.

However, she is supposedly in the company of Newt at the time the pigeon visits Credence. The scene at the church falls between the opening of Jacob's case in front of Graves at the wand permit office in MACUSA, and Newt and Tina back on the streets of the city to locate Jacob. It also is set in the script as the scene tag slips from "Day" to "Afternoon."

Tina could have slipped away from Newt briefly before they left, perhaps during a bathroom break, leaving him under someone else's guard. But it is not mentioned. However, we see in Scene 33 how easily Newt slips away briefly from her. Is this a clue that she could have done the same earlier?

Later, after escaping from MACUSA, the team lands on a rooftop overlooking the city where a pigeon coop is housed. As if to make sure we noticed the pigeon reference, Queenie reads Jacob's mind that his grandfather kept pigeons.

One of the cons against Tina as the pigeon is that she didn't transform to save herself during the execution scene. I could see this being explained away in a couple of ways—MACUSA could have protections against this sort of transformation, as Hogwarts did against apparating. Or, she could have hesitated to do, hoping to save Newt as well, until it was too late.

Whether the pigeon is Tina (my bet!) or another witch or wizard, I will be on the hunt for another sighting in the next movie.

One last thought—would a talented wizard who had a strong enough interest in animals to become a Magizoologist not also care enough to become an Animagi? Perhaps that's why Newt seems to understand their language so well.

Wizard Involvement in No-Maj Wars

Through her writing on MACUSA in Pottermore, Rowling tells us that the wizarding community doesn't necessarily take part in Muggle wars. During the Revolutionary War, witches and wizards across the land met to discuss "Country of Kind?" Should they unite with the No-Maj's in their fight for independence, or was their greater allegiance to the hidden international magical community?

While MACUSA decided this war was not their fight, many individuals ended up taking part, especially to protect their neighbors.

This discussion begs the question of how the wizarding community would choose to respond in a world war. We know that the Scamander brothers were both involved in WWI to some extent, but we don't yet know how involved the wizarding world was.

In Pottermore, Rowling has one line regarding the participation debate in the Revolutionary War that I feel will likely be revisited and play a crucial role in the upcoming series:

> Pro-interventionists argued that they might be able to save lives; anti-interventionists that wizards risked their own security by revealing themselves in battle.
> (Pottermore)

We know that MACUSA's biggest fear is revealing the magical community to the No-Maj. And we know that one of the arguments for the use of atomic weapons at the end of WWII was that they may be able to, in the end, save more lives than those lost.

I feel that we are headed for a scenario where wizards following Grindelwald will enter the war to exterminate as many Muggles as possible, and the rest of the wizarding world will be forced to participate to combat them.

Wizarding scientists, like Newt, will face an even more massive ethical dilemma: whether to use their powers (and beasts) to design weapons of mass destruction in hopes that, in the end, they may save more lives than they take.

The Death Sentence

When Graves sentences Newt and Tina to death, he tells the executioners to do it immediately and he will inform the president. But should they not have a trial?

Madam Picquery only ordered him to impound the case and arrest them. She said nothing about execution. In fact, she says to "Take them to the cells!" and hints at a trial with "We'll be the judges of that!" (p. 148)

It seems that Graves is acting on his own here. As such, we must assume that Grindelwald feels threatened by Newt. For what reason?

1) Possibly his connection to Albus Dumbledore.
2) That Newt knows and understands more about the Obscurus than Grindelwald does.
3) That Newt could blow his cover due to his slip up about "using" the Obscurus—"So it's useless without the host" (p. 159). Both Newt and Tina react strongly to this, looking at Graves in a new way.

With this final revelation, the viewer should fully realize that Graves is not the man he claims to be. Grindelwald seeks to find and control the Obscurus currently destroying New York. He will let nothing and no one stand in his way.

Grindelwald

If you've ever read a Harry Potter story, you know to start looking for clues early on regarding the villain in disguise. This was certainly true with Fantastic Beasts.

From the moment Graves steps onto the screen, observing the destruction of the Obscurus attack, we know he is different than the No-Majs around him. But not only is he keenly observant and knowledgeable, he's also intrigued. This unknown magical being capable of causing a wrath of destruction arouses his interest.

The first words out of Graves' mouth in the Major Investigation Department at MACUSA are:

> *I was there. This is a beast. No human could do what this thing is capable of, Madam President.* (p. 41)

He knows the power of the beast. He knows it's stronger than a wizard.

I want you to notice something else about the quote above. It comes immediately after Madam Picquery's: "They think this is related to Grindelwald's attacks in Europe" (41).

That's juxtaposition. One of Rowling's tricks for hiding a clue. That Graves speaks about the power of the beast immediately after Picquery talks of Grindelwald's attacks is the slyest of hints that there's a connection.

The clues increase as we progress through the film. Graves' clandestine meetings with Credence certainly rouses suspicion while reinforcing his personal interest in the Obscurus. But he's an Auror, a man whose job is to investigate exactly this sort of magical disturbance. Who would suspect the chief law enforcer of being the world's most wanted man? That's reverse expectations, another Rowling technique.

Where we start to see open chinks in his façade is in the interrogation scene. He doesn't like it when Newt protests: "I'm not one of Grindelwald's fanatics" (p. 158).

However, his greatest slipup is when he understands from Newt's description that the Obscurus is "useless without the host" (p. 159). *Useless.*

Newt, who would never think of using a parasitical killer, suddenly senses the dark, hidden nature of Graves, and Tina along with him. So, they must be eliminated.

From there, the clues start to pile up:

- Graves uses a fancy spell to lock his office. Wonder what, or *who*, he has locked in there? Fortunately, he underestimates non-magical power for simply breaking down a door.
- He calls Credence a Squib—wouldn't American wizards have a different word for them, as they do for Muggles?
- "Find the child and we'll all be free." (p. 89)—With these words to Credence, Graves confirms that he's after something a bit bigger than catching a beast run amok.

Grindelwald is all about harnessing power. He recognizes, like Newt, the extreme importance of these beasts—but he seeks to *use* them rather than *save* them. Just like he wants with Credence. Only Tina and Newt care about Credence's welfare. I hope this disturbed young man will recognize that in the end.

Because we all know Grindelwald will not remain in MACUSA prison for long.

Obscurus

We get the best definition of what an Obscurus is as, during the jail cell scene, Newt and Tina try to explain it to Jacob.

Tina

> *It's an unstable, uncontrollable Dark force that busts out and— and attacks . . . and then vanishes . . .* (p. 150-1)

Newt notes that it's the result of a magical child trying to hide their magical ability. Later, in the interrogation with Graves, he calls it a "parasitical magical force" (p. 160).

We also learn that, while more Obscurials existed in historic times when witches and wizards were openly persecuted, by the 1920s, they are rare. They also kill their host. The oldest survivor Newt knows of was ten.

Which sets up Modesty as the red herring perfectly. With Graves using Credence to find the Obscurial, and the young man's lack of knowledge regarding who it is, the viewer is lead to believe he could not be the one we are seeking. But his eight-year-old sister could.

One interesting structural setup Rowling uses to hint at the nature of the Obscurus is how she sandwiches the Team's capture of the escaped Occamy between Credence's killing of Mary Lou and then afterward, his betrayal from Graves and subsequent loss of control. For me, the purpose behind this is for the reader to subtly compare and contrast the care and intent behind Newt and Team's protection of a magical beast of truly monstrous proportions with Grindelwald's contempt and disregard for the young man whose power he cannot even recognize.

However, there is something more. As the Occamy can grow or shrink to fit its container, as does the Obscurus. For most of the story, it hides within Credence's small, human body. But when rage activates it, it swells into a horrific storm capable of destroying an entire city.

One of Rowling's most powerful, beautifully dark verses describing this power:

**The Obscurus moves horribly beneath Credence's skin.
An awful inhuman growl comes out of his mouth, from which something dark begins to bloom. (p. 230)**

To bloom. We've only just begun.

Finally, I'd like to note some of the wording Rowling uses to describe the bits and pieces of blown-up Obscurus:

Only small tatters of black matter are left— floating through the air like feathers. (p. 253)

She also uses "black snowlike particles" (p. 238) and refers to him as a *Dark force* (p. 249). While showing this "black matter" floating up to "reconnect with its host" hints strongly that something of Credence survives, it also hints of the *atomic* nature of the Obscurus. With an *imploding* explosion, its elements are broken apart. Its broken matter is blown about like light particles of fallout dust.

For this magical bomb, however, even when its matter may be divided and its energy spent, the dark force which binds it can rejoin…for perhaps a greater explosion later.

The Elder Wand

We know the Elder Wand will figure into Fantastic Beasts somehow, some way. We're just not sure of the timing.

Per canon, somewhere between 1899 – 1945, Grindelwald stole it from the wandmaker Gregorovitch, stunning him in the process to claim the allegiance of this most powerful wand. In 1945, Dumbledore won the wand off Grindelwald when they dueled. However, for the exact timing of Grindelwald's claim, we only know that it was as he rose to power.

Two key questions present themselves:

- Does Grindelwald already possess the Elder Wand during this first movie?

- If the wand owes its allegiance to Grindelwald at the movie's beginning, does it still by the movie's end?

I believe that Grindelwald *is* in possession of the wand at the beginning set in Europe. The previously unknown powerful spell that he casts, which kills five Aurors at once with a white flash of light, is meant to hint at this.

We do not see Graves using the Elder Wand throughout the course of the movie, because to do so would make Graves' friends and co-workers question why he suddenly has a new wand. However, from established canon, the wand does not need to physically change hands for its loyalty to switch to the witch or wizard who disarms its owner.

The truly murky question comes about the ending, the scene in the subway. Newt shoots out a spell which lashes around Grindelwald like a whip, making him lose balance and drop his wand. Graves' wand. Tina immediately *Accios* it.

Did Newt disarm Grindelwald? Or did Tina?

Fandom is already debating the nuances of this bit of wand lore. But I believe: Why not both?

Teamwork, and not going it alone, has always been a crucial theme for Rowling. She will be eager to explore a new depth to the elements of power and corruption that the Elder Wand represents. She will not wish to merely repeat what we have seen before through Draco's disarming of Dumbledore in Harry Potter.

So why not add the dimension of a team disarmament? It would be quite fitting with the WWII theme as well.

Except there is the complication that we know Grindelwald has possession of the wand when Dumbledore disarms him in 1945. However, we also know Dumbledore to be the master of manipulation.

Here's my best guess of what Rowling is doing with the Elder Wand. She's adding nuance to its lore. If the wand owner is defeated in a team effort, then the wand splits its loyalty. Both Newt and Tina have a claim to the Elder Wand, but neither can claim it as their own without the other.

Because the wand no longer responds to him, though he is still in physical possession, Grindelwald goes on a mad rampage throughout the series to find and kill Newt, totally discounting Tina's contribution…just as he has all along.

Dumbledore, however, understands. Knowing that the odds of Tina and Newt being able to claim the wand and defeat Grindelwald are low due to its split loyalty, Dumbledore offers up a plan. If Grindelwald overpowers Newt, perhaps a pretend death, and wins back the part that was loyal to Newt, would the wand then be ineffective in a battle that included Tina, still part owner, unbeknownst to Grindelwald?

If Newt can use elements from his Beasts to wipe out a city full of memories, I'm sure he can come up with something to brew a version of the Draught of Living Death.

Thus would explain Grindelwald's:

Will we die, just a little. (p. 257)

He knows one of them must die in loyalty to the Elder Wand.

Deleted Scene

There is a deleted scene from the end movie that shows Credence on a ship leaving NY[11]. As such, we can be sure that he lived.

As we know that Tom Riddle was born on December 31, 1926, many fans are speculating that Credence is on his way to London and may somehow end up at the orphanage and affect Riddle's birth in some way.

While the timeline is ripe for this speculation as the first movie takes place in December 1926 (see Timeline in World Building), I personally don't see Credence hurrying to an orphanage in London. I think one of the reasons for this assumption is that the movie Credence looks so young, but the script book describes him as an adult. My guess is that Credence may be tracking Grindelwald, who betrayed him.

Looking Forward

Based on my analysis of the initial film, here are what is shaping up to be the key mystery questions of the series:

- How much destruction will Credence bring about at the manipulation of Grindelwald before Newt and Team disarm him?

- How many wizards and No-Maj will die before Grindelwald is defeated?

- Will Newt have to die, *just a little*, for the Elder Want to be fully stripped from Grindelwald's possession?

Whatever his motives or destination, I'm sure that we will see Credence again, and that he will probably affect the setup for the future Harry Potter story.

---

[11] http://www.cinemablend.com/news/1586630/fantastic-beasts-ending-a-key-scene-that-was-cut-and-why

Secret Five

Inside Newt's Case

(The Beasts)

In *Fantastic Beasts and Where to Find Them*, the beasts are the stars of the show. Rowling has collected creatures from a variety of locations and cultures and given them her own unique spin. Many are magical beasts of her own creation. Rowling constructs each one to be as individual and quirky as her human cast.

Newt is our medium for understanding these special creatures. He is a scientist and conservationist who seeks to protect his friends from those who would destroy them. Whether he is a true Dr. Dolittle or not, he also seems to possess the ability to understand their hearts and their needs...and maybe their language.

Beasts Listed in Order of Appearance:

Dougal the Demiguise

Dougal is the first of Newt's beasts mentioned, when he quickly closes a latch on his case that has flipped open. He brings the case on his lap and whispers to Dougal to settle down. Throughout the story, Dougal seems particularly impatient to get out of that case.

Demiguises hail from the Far East, and have the ability to become invisible. Its pelt is highly prized as the hairs can be spun into an Invisibility Cloak (FB2001, p. 9). One popular fan theory was that Dumbledore possessed an Invisibility Cloak of his own, which is why he was so good at knowing what all was going about Hogwarts. If this were the case, is it possible that Newt may have attained the Demiguise pelt for Dumbledore?

As he is a protector of wildlife, he could have attained the pelt from a dead Demiguise, or simply collected enough hairs shed from his own living one. One thing is for certain…we must wonder if Newt has obtained a cloak for himself. However, since Harry is associated with the Invisibility Cloak, I think Rowling may do something different for Newt.

Even though Dougal is the first beast mentioned and we hear about him frequently throughout the story, we do not see him until near the end, through the window at Macy's:

> "…a silvery-haired orangutan-like creature, with a curious, wizened face—clambering over a display to reach a box of sweets." (p. 207)

While Rowling also describes the Demiguise as a peaceful herbivore, Newt warns his friends that they can "give a nasty nip if provoked." (p. 207) But perhaps its most intriguing feature is its ability to foresee the immediate probable future. When the Demiguise is experiencing a premonition, its eyes turn blue, as Dougal's do when he is correctly predicting the bedlam that occurs from Queenie stepping on the Christmas tree ornament.

Dougal's eyes will bear watching throughout the series.

Regarding his name, Dougal is Gaelic and means black stranger. I would imagine that with his ability to disappear, the Demiguise would appear quite dark and mysterious to most.

One other thing to note: in *Cursed Child*, Albus and Scorpius use Tincture of Demiguise to write an invisible note to be revealed to Harry in the future, therefore he will know where to rescue them.

Niffler

While the Niffler gets the most screen time, it's one of Newt's least dangerous creatures…aside from getting Newt arrested. Described as a "furry black cross between a mole and a duck-billed platypus" (p. 14), Newt's Niffler wins the cute factor. He also has a predilection for pilfering everything glittery, which keeps Newt in a lot of trouble. From a beggar's hat to a dog collar to a jewelry store, if it glitters, he wants it.

It almost seems the Niffler's sole role in the film is to cause wild, crazy action while looking adorable. But this is JK Rowling we're talking about.

Nifflers do have one other quality—they are great diggers and will tunnel deep within the earth in search of treasure. We know the Nazis liked to tunnel themselves, whether to find or store treasure, to create bunkers, or for other military advantages. Perhaps the Niffler will prove more useful than troublesome to Newt and Team in the coming films. Especially if Newt had a whole family of them.

If you'd like to see an animal that may have inspired the Niffler, check out this CNN report on a newborn puggle (see footnote), which Rowling retweeted on November 21, 1016. [12]

Occamy

Native to the Far East and India, the Occamy is a "small, blue, snake-like bird" (p. 24). Their shells are made of silver, which makes them rather aggressive as they are always on the defense against human greed.

Perhaps the Occamy imprints as well since the one that hatches in the bank, that Jacob had kept in his pocket, becomes Jacob's Occamy. Newt reintroduces them inside his case. I'm sure having a scary serpent-bird on your side, one who can expand to an enormous size, could come in handy.

Which brings up the Occamy's most intriguing characteristic: they are choranaptyxic. In tracing this word of Rowling's creation, I come up with:

Chora—*Khôra* in ancient Greek is usually defined as a site, space, or receptacle, but for Plato, the term also held philosophical meaning:

"In Plato's account, *khôra* is neither being nor nonbeing but an interval between in which the "forms" were originally held; it "gives space" and has maternal overtones (a womb, matrix)[13]

I believe *tyxic* comes from the Greek *tyxia*, which means to pour. All of which fits perfectly together for the Occamy as it seems to pour into the receptacle it inhabits.

Based on the Plato above, the Occamy thus acts as something that flows between forms, being neither solely solid nor solely liquid. It forces us to consider the nature of matter and of being, to consider that not all of life is a *this* or *that*, fitting within a simple dualistic designation, but can expand beyond our understanding.

Another insight into the Occamy is the possible link to Occam's Razor. This principle, used in both science and philosophy, basically states that when considering theories to explain a principle, the simpler one is usually

---

[12] http://www.cnn.com/2016/11/21/world/puggle-birth-taronga-zoo/index.html

[13] https://en.wikipedia.org/wiki/Kh%C3%B4ra

the best. Perhaps Rowling is giving us a guide for interpreting her clues!

I'm curious as to how the Occamies expand and contract. Inside Newt's case, they are of a size that does not take up the whole space. May we assume he has some sort of spell on them? Or possibly the Occamy itself controls the size it becomes, because when we see its blue tail slither into the department store attic window, shortly after seeing its invisible babysitter eat an apple and a lollipop, it seems to be of a normal size. At least not of the size to attract No-Maj attention.

The 2001 *Fantastic Beasts* textbook says they reach a maximum length of fifteen feet, so I guess they couldn't squash the whole world.

Finally, I think Rowling may hint at something a bit more personal through the Occamy as well. Perhaps because the saying "a tempest in a teapot" goes through my mind whenever I think of the Occamy, I associate them with worry. Worry, in a way, grows to the size of its receptacle, the space you allow it in your heart and your mind.

For now, I'm worrying how this adorable beast could be misused in the hands of a dark wizard wanting to harness its powers.

Pickett the Bowtruckle

Bowtruckles are tree guardians who are green and look "part stick insect, part plant" (p. 25). Newt's favored Bowtruckle is named Pickett and lives in his breast pocket throughout the course of the film as he has "attachment issues." We also find out later that Pickett had been sick and needed the extra body warmth.

Unfortunately, this closeness Newt has with Pickett makes him picked on (pun!) by the other Bowtruckles inside Newt's case. Named Poppy, Titus, Marlow, Finn, and Tom, I feel sure that there's some significance in these names but can come up with nothing more than literary characters. Finn and Tom could be Huck Finn and Tom Sawyer. Titus may be inspired by *Titus Andronicus* by Shakespeare. Marlow could be the playwright and poet Christopher Marlowe. And Poppy could be Rowling's own Madam Poppy Pomfrey, the nurse at Hogwarts.

Fortunately, Pick (Newt's pet name for Pickett) is quite skilled at picking locks. Which comes in handy in saving Newt and Tina from the death pool. But then gets Pickett traded to Gnarlak for information on Newt's lost Demiguise.

I'm hoping Pickett's name is derived more from his skill as a locksmith than being picked on. Surely that skill will come in handy again.

Puffskein, Appaloosa

This favored wizard pet is mentioned twice as Newt's reason for being in New York—to buy for a birthday gift. The only breeder of the Appaloosa variety lives in New York. Except, he no longer breeds these cute little furballs, having been stopped by MACUSA a year before.

Newt's desired Puffskein, which never appears onscreen, seems a bit like a short intro MacGuffin to me. Rowling is very aware of this literary device, having named her weatherman in Philosopher's/Sorcerer's Stone MacGuffin.

Billywig

Hailing from Australia, these little insects pack a most interesting sting.

Those who have been stung by a Billywig suffer giddiness followed by levitation. (2001FB, p. 4)

...an effect that wizarding teens in Australia seem to seek out for fun.

In the film, the escaped Billywigs serve as an alert to Newt, letting him know of their escape from his case...and therefore the possibility of others. With their "helicopter-like wings on its head" (p. 56), and the way they fly about so quickly, you could almost imagine them like a drone. I wonder if they have a way of communicating to Newt whatever they see?

Finally, I'd like to note that these magical insects are a "vivid sapphire blue" (FB2001, p. 4)—another running bit. For more, see the White and Blue section in the Plot chapter.

Murtlap

Described as "—a ratlike creature with an anemone-style growth on its back" (p. 51), Newt's Murtlap is the first animal to escape from his case when Jacob opens it and bites him on the neck.

According the 2001 *Fantastic Beasts* textbook, Murtlap growths "promote resistance to curses and jinxes" (p. 30). The bite causes Jacob to retch and sweat and twitch. But at least he doesn't have the worst reaction, as Newt notes...flames shooting out of his anus.

When Jacob touches his fingers to the Murtlap bite on his neck in the epilogue scene, I have to wonder if the protective qualities of the Murtlap's back growth helped preserve a snippet of his magical memories.

Swooping Evil

Swooping Evil is a beast created for the film that did not appear in the 2001 *Fantastic Beasts* textbook. As such it deserves intense scrutiny as

Rowling will have had a specific purpose in creating it.

When we first meet Swooping Evil it is in the form of its spiny cocoon, with Newt milking it for its "luminous venom" (p. 98). Newt's been studying whether a diluted potion of it will remove bad memories.

Newt flings the Swooping Evil at Jacob, operating it as a sort of yo-yo:

The creature bursts out from its cocoon— a bat-like, spiky, colorful creature— and howls in Jacob's face before Newt recalls it. (p. 99)

Swooping Evil must remain a calm creature when ensconced within its cocoon as Newt seems to carry it around in his coat. Fortunately, that means the beast is available for rescues, which happens three times.

The first is in the Pool of Death scene to help Tina escape. When Newt flings the Evil, it expands into a "gigantic, spooky, but weirdly beautiful butterfly-esque reptile with skeletal wings" (p. 170). After saving Tina, it folds back into a cocoon in Newt's hand.

Shortly after, as Newt and Tina are dodging curses from Aurors in MACUSA's basement, Newt uses the Evil to save them once more. When it sticks its proboscis into an Auror's ear, Newt commands it to leave the brains. Sounds like a tasty treat…with serious potential for inflicting damage.

One last time Newt calls on the Evil to save them, in the shoot-out with Grindelwald in the end when Evil emerges from its cocoon to shield Newt, giving him time to reach for his wand and cast a spell. This causes Grindelwald to drop his wand and for quick-thinking Tina to *Accio* it.

Without Swooping Evil, they may never have stopped and caught Grindelwald. And without its venom, which Newt diluted and had Frank spread in the storm, the No-Maj of New York would still be aware of everything that transpired. And Grindelwald would have the war he desires.

When Grindelwald escapes, my guess is that with his interest in powerful beasts, he will be seeking to relieve Newt of his yo-yo bird. Swooping Evil also highlights another aspect that I believe will play out profoundly through the series—Newt does not mind using his creatures as weapons of defense.

One little tidbit to consider: one of the planes involved in the bombing of Hiroshima on August 6, 1945 was called Necessary Evil. It's a stretch, I admit, but worth noting.

Frank the Thunderbird

The Thunderbird did not appear in the 2001 *Fantastic Beasts* textbook. It's a creature Rowling borrowed from various Native Americans, among them the Algonquin. According to their beliefs, the Thunderbird had a link with the Horned Serpent, another creature Rowling borrowed. The Thunderbird ruled the world above and the Horned Serpent the world below. (For more on the original beliefs see http://www.native-languages.org/algonquian-legends.htm).

Rowling's version looks like "a large albatross, its glorious wings shimmering with cloud- and sunlike patterns" (p. 100). The flapping of Frank's wings causes a thunderstorm, rain and lightning included. It seems the storms he causes are linked to his own emotional state because as Newt calms him, the sunshine returns.

Rowling uses a beautiful blending of storm and sun imagery in describing the Thunderbird. He is truly a majestic creature, and one Newt is quite fond of. Freeing Frank is the real reason Newt came to the US. (At least we think he is.) (p. 101)

Frank is the one animal in his case that Newt is extremely relieved to see still present. He comments that the Thunderbird getting loose would be "catastrophic."

As for Frank's name, I'm sure Rowling had someone in mind. The possibility that intrigues me the most is Franklin D Roosevelt, the US president for most of WWII and the one who ordered the Manhattan Project to build the world's first atomic bomb.

One piece of evidence that points to Roosevelt is the location of Frank's wounds from his captivity in Egypt: his leg. Roosevelt suffered from paralysis due to polio.

With the Thunderbird's ability to produce a vast storm, Newt's fear that it could cause a catastrophe, and Frank's possible link to Roosevelt, I'm afraid we will see him again by series end. It's very possible Frank could be used as a weapon of mass destruction (see the Forecast chapter for more).

Doxys

Doxys are mentioned flying around twice inside Newt's case, but Rowling gives very little of their description, except that they buzz around Jacob's head. In the 2001 Fantastic Beasts book, she describes them as a biting fairy.

> Like the fairy, it has a miniature human form, though in the Doxy's case this is covered in thick black hair and has an extra pair of arms and legs. (FB2001, p. 10)

I mostly mention them here to keep track of in case they have a more prominent role in the next story.

Dung Beetle

Dung Beetles are not mentioned in the 2001 *Fantastic Beasts* book, but they appear at least twice in the movie inside Newt's case and are mentioned specifically in the book as they go past Jacob rolling their dung. I almost shouted out in the movie when I saw them as I've been tracking Egyptian mythological references within the Harry Potter series for years, and dung beetles are one of the mythiest.

Because of its nature to roll giant balls of dung across huge distances by navigating via the sun, and that its young would appear to be born magically from this ball, the scarab was associated with life, resurrection, and the sun. Thousands of scarab amulets have been found in Egyptian burials, showing how widely these little critters were worshiped.

They have a link to alchemy as well. For some alchemists, they were a symbol of the process of putrefaction and fermentation.

Graphorn

> "built like a saber-toothed tiger but with slimy tentacles at its mouth" (p. 103).

The Graphorns are large and aggressive, but seem to have a fondness for Newt (FB2001, p. 19), nuzzling him affectionately.

The family that Newt carries in his case seems to suit two purposes:

1) As they are the last couple of breeding Graphorns in existence, and have already reproduced, they represent Newt's conservation interest and abilities.

2) Because of that unusual and fearsome appearance, Jacob is initially afraid of them. But he conquers his fear and reaches out to stroke the head of their calf. A very important test for his friendship with Newt.

They would make an awesome force in a wizarding war, wouldn't they?

Fwooper

The Fwooper appears briefly in the scene of Newt and Jacob feeding the animals in his case.

This bird hails from Africa and exists in many vibrant colors. The current one in Newt's case is a bright pink. Newt must have an excellent silencing charm on his, because the Fwooper's song is known to drive people insane (FB2001, p. 18).

Golden Leaves, Glow Bugs, and Grindylows

This is a fascinating reference in the script book. As Jacob explores Newt's case, we see:

> golden "leaves" falling from a tiny tree, which move together en masse toward the camera. They swarm upward, mingling with Doxys, Glow Bugs, and Grindylows, which float through the air. (p. 110)

Doxys received their own heading as they are mentioned twice, but the golden "leaves," Glow Bugs, and Grindylows are only mentioned this once.

Only the Grindylows appear in the 2001 *Fantastic Beasts* textbook. We know these water demons best from *Goblet of Fire* where they appear in the Merpeople challenge to attack Harry and the other Champions. For the Glow Bugs and Golden "Leaves," we only have the description above.

To me, it's clear from Rowling's "quoting" of "leaves," that she is using *leaves* as a figure of speech, an analogy. These leaves are something else; **they are alive**.

It's hard to tell exactly what she's doing with the Grindylows in this brief description, but in the film you can see clearly that they are floating in bubbles of water. Why have the Grindylows floating in air? Why not have a little pond somewhere in the case? She's had the appropriate environment for every other beast.

With Rowling, every choice has a reason. And here, I think she's going for a sum of the whole, a powerful symbol when these four *elements* are viewed together, almost as one.

Elemental Representation of these Living Creatures
- Golden Leaves—**Earth**, as they are part of a tree
- Doxys—**Air**
- Glow Bugs—**Fire**. As the glow represents fire
- Grindylows—**Water**

But there's one more element here. It's that unification of these beasts together. It's the reason the Grindylows are floating; we can understand that we are to join these four as one. The fifth element—Quintessence.

Five is the magical number for this series. The Golden Leaves fall from a small tree and swarm together in a mass, joining with the other beasts. Rowling shows the viewer a beautiful reimagined image for the Tree of Life. Those golden "leaves" become birds or butterflies, both of which are powerful symbols frequently used for spirit.

So, Rowling has created here a very short reference that hints at one of her prime theme for the series—Spirit or Soul—living here in Newt's case.

Nundu

The Nundu is a lion-like creature hailing from East Africa (a running bit) that only appears once in the script book. Newt is shown feeding his as it stands on a rock and roars at the moon.

However, the Nundus has more written about it not only in the 2001 *Fantastic Beasts* book, but also Pottermore.

Magic Abilities
Moves silently in spite of its size, and its breath causes disease which can eliminate entire villages

Dangers
Arguably the most dangerous beast in the world due to its deadly breath (Pottermore)

Newt did seem anxious not to remain in the beast's presence for long. That breath must really stink.

The 2001 text book says it takes at least 100 wizards to subdue one (FB2001, p. 31). Yet Newt clearly has one in his suitcase.

Newt must be one heck of a wizard.

Diricawl

The Diricawl appears briefly in the scene of Newt and Jacob feeding the animals in his case.

Diricawl is the wizard name of the dodo bird, whose home is on the Indian Ocean island of Mauritius (FB2001, p. 9). The No-Maj believe the bird is extinct, but this is due to the Diricawl's ability to Disapparate and reappear elsewhere. As they are a flightless bird, this is their main method of protection. Indeed, in Newt's case, the mother's chicks are constantly Apparating about her.

As a dodo bird appears in *Alice's Adventures in Wonderland* by Lewis Carroll, and Rowling has drawn on this work before in the Harry Potter series, we may want to watch out for future appearances from this Diricawl.

Mooncalf

First hint we have of these is the crate of mooncalf pellets that Jacob sits on when he first enters Newt's suitcase.

These friendly, gentle creatures are described as "shy, with huge eyes filling their whole faces" (p. 111). Jacob's tender and caring feeding of them is a sort of test for Newt.

Per the 2001 *Fantastic Beasts* book, they emerge only on the full moon and their mating dance is what's responsible for the mysterious crop circles (p. 29). Their dung is also a great fertilizer for a magical garden. Wonder if Newt is growing anything special?

Unnamed Creature

In the script, Rowling shows Newt feeding a "luminescent creature with sprouting alien-like tendrils" (p. 111). His careful feeding with a bottle marks it as an infant.

I could find no reference to this creature in the 2001 *Fantastic Beasts* book. Perhaps it is a new creation for the film series. And perhaps we'll see it in toddler form in the next movie.

Dragons—Ukrainian Ironbellies

This special breed of dragon is mentioned only once in the text. Newt worked with them on the Eastern Front in WWI. But Harry Potter fans will recognize the Ironbelly from its star performance in *Deathly Hallows*. It was the dragon chained in the bowels of Gringott's which Hermione freed to help the Trio escape.

As noted in the 2001 *Fantastic Beasts* textbook, this largest of dragons is capable of carrying off an entire ship. Newt's war experience surely shows that he's well aware of their capability to be weaponized.

To me, the name Ironbellies hints at a tank.

Erumpent

Hailing from Africa (a running bit), the Erumpent looks like a rhinoceros with a massive horn sticking out of its forehead. In *Deathly Hallows*, the Lovegoods have an Erumpent horn mounted on their wall, thinking it belonged to the mythical Crumple-Horned Snorkack. When Harry, Hermione, and Ron attempted to escape from Xenophilius, his stun charm set off the horn with a powerful explosion that destroyed most of his house.

Imagine the possible danger from one of these creatures in season and let loose on an unsuspecting city searching for a mate.

Newt's Erumpent happens to be five times the size of the rhino she's eager to mate with…who is terrified of her. But notice that five again—another running bit through this book.

Beside her massive size, the Erumpent horn is powerful. Glowing orange when she is aroused, it also liquefies a tree, turning it into glowing bubbles before it explodes. As seen by the destruction of the Lovegood home and the havoc Newt's pet wreaks at the Central Park Zoo, an Erumpent would make a powerful weapon.

Rowling's careful showing of the destruction this creature is capable of hints that we may see her again in future movies. She is also one of the beasts Jacob remembers and turns into a pastry at his new shop.

Erumpent is a word pre-Rowling that means "bursting forth or through a surface" usually used in biology.[14]

Ashwinder

The Ashwinder is only mentioned once, and then only for its egg. In Newt's negotiations with Gnarlak for information regarding the location of his lost Demiguise, he offers up a frozen Ashwinder egg. On must wonder how and why Newt is carrying a frozen egg in his coat pocket? How many other creatures does he have lurking about him?

Ashwinders are born of a magical fire left unattended. They will slither through the building and leave a nest of bright red eggs. These eggs are so hot that they can set fire to whatever they're near if not frozen immediately. One frozen, the eggs can be used in love potions (FB2001, p. 2). Wonder who Gnarlak is seeking to entrance?

Anyway, it's nice to know that Newt has some high-powered fire bombs at his disposal. Or, if his charms fail him, he has another way of making Tina fall for him!

Lethifold

The Lethifold, mentioned in the 2001 *Fantastic Beasts* textbook, does not appear in the movie. But it is hinted at…slightly.

The Lethifold is a nightmare of a beast, a silent killer that attacks people in their sleep. It is described as resembling a "black cloak perhaps half an inch thick (thicker if it has recently killed and digested a victim),

---

[14] https://en.oxforddictionaries.com/definition/us/erumpent

which glides along the ground at night" (2001FB, p. 25).

In the textbook, Rowling details a story about a Lethifold attack on the drowsing wizard, Flavius Belby, which takes place in Papau New Guinea. Fortunately, Belby is able to beat off the Lethifold through his Patronus.

The Patronus was a crucial spell throughout the Potter series from the time it was introduced in *Prisoner of Azkaban*. In the *Fantastic Beasts* movie, we've not yet seen the Patronus or the Lethifold, but there is a slight hint.

When Tina is hauling Newt into her office MACUSA after her embarrassing shut-out in front of Madam Picquery and her old boss Graves, she mentions that Newt was just in Equatorial Guinea. Note: It's not shown how she knows this, whether Newt informed her in a conversation offscreen or if she's examined his passport. However she found out, Newt alludes to having been there for field research.

Equatorial Guinea is located in central Africa (see Films and Locations in the Forecast chapter). Papau New Guinea forms half of the island of New Guinea, an island in the Pacific Ocean north of Australia. These countries only have the name Guinea in common. They are not in the same continent or even location of the world. But sometimes that link of name is enough for Rowling to start her fans' minds churning (like mine!).

Newt tells Tina that he has just completed a year of field research for his book. We know this book includes the Lethifold. As Lethifolds live in tropical climates only, could Newt have gone through a region like Papau New Guinea as well and collected one? We've seen, quite clearly through the Erumpent and Nundu that he is unafraid of collecting beasts that terrorize others.

Later in the film, through Grindelwald's intense interests in the Occamy, we get the sense that he may be interested in acquiring the powers of magical creatures which far outstrips that of witches and wizards. Wouldn't the Lethifold be a prized beast for him to acquire? Think of the terror he could spread through an army of creatures that can silently murder people in their sleep.

Runespoor

The Runespoor does not appear in the text of the script book for Fantastic Beasts. I include it here due to its prominent placement on the cover.

According to the 2001 textbook, Runespoors, native to Burkina Faso in Africa, are serpents with three heads.

Although the Runespoor can be associated with Dark wizards, what I find most intriguing about it is the nature of its three heads. From an observer's point of view, the left head of the serpent is the planner. This is the head that is analytical and plots its next move. The middle is the dreamer, often lost in its own fantasies and daydreams. And the right head is the critic, offering a continuous criticism of the other two. Its bite is "extremely venomous" (FB2001, p. 37).

There are many ways to interpret the similarities of these three heads to people and society. However, Rowling offers two clues that I find fascinating—the Runespoor's left and middle head frequently team up to bite off the right head, and its eggs are used in potions to "stimulate mental agility." This description speaks to me as a writer.

1) Within the writer, there is the side who must dream up the stories, the side that must handle the logical end of both writing and selling the work, and then the ever-present sense of failure, both the creative side as well as the marketing. We flow constantly between these aspects of ourselves as we seek to channel our inner creativity and present it to the world. That inner critic can often have a poisonous and painful effect on both the creative and business endeavors.

2) In the publishing world, there are the writers (the dreamers), the agents and editors (the plotters), and reviewers and bloggers (the critics). It would not be uncommon on some particularly bad days for the writers and the people who represent them to wish to band together to silence their critics.

Alas, the writer needs both the critic inside her own head as well as the ones outside it.

As to how Rowling may be using the Runespoor in Fantastic Beasts, it adds to the list of Africa hints. I feel we may very well go on Safari before the series' end.

Looking Forward

We've met so many magnificent animals. Whether dangerous or not, each one a special creature existing in the Garden of Eden of Newt's case.

I fear for them all. In the dark days that are sure to come, I feel Newt's creatures will be used and manipulated, just like Credence. And some, perhaps, killed.

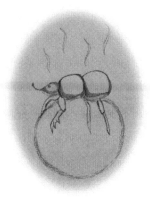

Secret Six

Rowling A Myth

(Myths and Ancient Beliefs)

The amount of alchemy that Rowling alluded to throughout Harry Potter has been well attested by both analysts and the author herself. For Fantastic Beasts, however, I feel she has something different in mind. Aside from one "thank Paracelsus" oath from Newt (p. 101), most of the allusions I've detected lead elsewhere.

In weaving myths into her subtext, Rowling draws from an international Muse. Throughout this guide, we see hints from the Egyptian dung beetles (covered in Beasts), to Biblical imagery of the Garden of Eden, to Greek myths such as the Trojan War, to the Native American Thunderbird (Beasts) to fairy tales like Sleeping Beauty (mentioned in Shipping).

In this section, we'll look at several of these mythical, folklore, and religious allusions to understand how she may be using them for this first movie...and then where and how they will carry us forward.

Garden of Eden

Though not extensive, Garden of Eden imagery teases the reader within *Fantastic Beasts*. Inside Newt's case, the animals are well cared for, existing peacefully within their domain, in a sense of innocence and paradise...one that a few seek to escape from. We even have a Tree of Life when you consider the Golden Leaves (as discussed in the Beasts chapter), with a serpent-bird Occamy on guard nearby.

Outside of the case, an angel watches carefully in the form of Seraphina Picquery. She is most anxious to keep the gates of this garden closed.

For the writer of Genesis, Eden lies in the East. When Jacob fully opens the case, it is in his home in the Lower East Side.

I can see how the hint of the Garden of Eden would appeal to Rowling. The innocence of humanity before the fall contrasts strongly against the depravity World War II unleashes.

Unfortunately, as we know from the Hebrew Bible myth, once those gates are closed, we can never return.

Trojan War

The Trojan War as described by Homer in the *Iliad* was considered by modern academics to be a legend, a myth. Until the ruins of Troy were discovered along the Aegean coast of Turkey by amateur German archaeologist Heinrich Schliemann and his Greek wife Sophia in 1871-2.

Rowling has given several hints toward Troy and its war through names she chose for her characters:.

- **Leta/Leda** (Lestrange)—the mother of Helen of Troy
- **Theseus** (Scamander)—abducted Helen of Troy in her youth, which led partly to the Trojan War (see Theseus in the Character chapter for more). Also, his son Acamas hid in the Trojan horse.
- **Scamander**—name of a river that runs near Troy and a river god that fought on the Trojan side.
- **Artemis** (Newt's middle name)—goddess revered in Anatolia, with a temple that was a Wonder of the Ancient World, who participated in the Trojan War on the Trojan's side.

The Scamander reference is one that intrigues me the most because it hints that Rowling may have well imagined this Troy link to Newt's story from his character's initial conception.

As we know Fantastic Beasts will span the years of Hitler's rise to power and WWII, it's fair to assume that Rowling may draw parallels between this modern world war and its more ancient counterpart. If so, what would they be?

I believe the wrath of Achilles may be one fair comparison. Achilles is the strongest warrior in the Achaian army and the central character in the

Iliad. The story and the war largely revolve around his anger at the way he is treated, his sense of being cast out from his society, and his return to it. As such, I see hints that may link Achilles to Credence. Credence is disenfranchised from both societies he has links to—the No-Maj that call him a freak, and the wizards whom he prosecutes but longs to be part of. Graves/Grindelwald promises to bring him into this magical community, then betrays him.

In the next film, Credence may initially draw even further from all wizards as his wrath against what Grindelwald and the Aurors did engulfs him. By series end, however, I hope we will find him reunited with his wizarding family and healed. Probably through the efforts of Newt and Tina united, though I suspect Modesty will find her way back to her older brother as well. I just hope they protect his heels.

The *Iliad* is rich with meaning, and our series just begun, that I cannot adequately cover all the implications between it and Rowling's work at this point. I feel this will be a fruitful area of discovery, however, and hope that you will join me in exploring its mysteries on my blog. See Where Do We Go From Here for more information in the Appendix below.

Gordian Knot

The Gordian Knot was a dilemma presented to Alexander the Great on his way to conquering the world. It was a puzzle established by a humbler man who was given the kingship of a local area in Anatolia, now present-day Turkey. In seeking to rule the area, Alexander was forced to solve the riddle of how to untie this very complicated knot. Instead, he did the ancient equivalent of thinking outside the box. Bypassing the time-consuming process of searching for loose ends, he simply sliced through it or, per a different version, pulled out the post it was tied to.

The Gordian Knot has since become symbolic of a complex problem that may have a simple solution if one can think differently than others. It could rightly also be seen as a means to power. Both are fitting meanings for the powerful and cunning Slytherin's brooch.

Rowling's Gordian Knot was found in one continent and came to fruition in another. It was discovered amid the charred remains of Isolt Sayre's Pureblood family home in Ireland and became the emblem of the mixed-blood home she established in the New World. The brooch was a relic of Slytherin that came to grace an international school of witches and wizards founded to be inclusive of all.

I feel quite sure that there's more to the Gordian Knot brooch then we have yet seen. It will be interesting to watch what becomes of it in future books. While I doubt very seriously that it is a Horcrux, I do feel sure it contains some powerful magic that has not yet been fully revealed.

What is most interesting with the Gordian Knot and with the Slytherin side of the story here, is how Rowling is twisting Slytherin for this new book (covered more in the Theme chapter).

Pentagram

It intrigues me greatly to see the pentagram mosaic on the floor of MACUSA. With Rowling, symbols usually have great power and meaning. The pentagram both parallels and contrasts the Deathly Hallows symbol which is also in this movie. What could the pentagram tell us of where Rowling is going with Fantastic Beasts?

The pentagram is an ancient symbol that held meaning for various cultures and philosophers before it became associated with witches in more recent history.

One of these philosophers was Pythagoras, who has already been mentioned in Harry Potter. It is possible that Rowling is drawing on the belief of Pythagorians, whom I'll discuss more below. But the ancient philosopher who intrigues me most is Pherecydes of Syros.

For either of these men, the pentagram represented the "five recesses" of air, earth, fire, and water flowing into the fifth, spirit or quintessence.

When Tina enters the Pentagram Office and sets down Newt's case, she does so at the base of one of these "recesses," one of the five start points. Newt emerges from his case here. From the camera angle showing the top point of the pentagram, Newt emerges at the base of the fifth recess, Spirit.

It's just like Rowling to insert the symbol for the series as a floor mosaic. I believe that the pentagram with its ancient meaning will serve as the frame for this series like alchemy did in Harry Potter. If so, each movie may represent one of these five parts.

This first movie was water. With the importance of the water in the death chamber scene and the rain wiping out the memories at the end, water played an important role in this story.

Next, I want to discuss more about ancient beliefs about the pentagram through the philosophies of Pherecydes and Pythagoras.

Pherecydes

Pherecydes and Pythagoras are both Greek thinkers from the 6th century BCE who developed a related cosmology. About ten years older, many consider Pherecydes to have been a teacher to Pythagoras.

Pherecydes devised a cosmology built on the principle of five. They were five primordial forces in the world that lived in five recesses of the world. These five principles are believed to be the traditional earth, air, water, and fire but with a fifth principle added, sometimes referred to as aether, or spirit.

Much of the work of Pherecydes is lost, however snippets survive through references in ancient sources. As such a basic understanding of his beliefs and cosmology has been put together.

According to these beliefs, a war was brewing between the gods, the forces that control the world. The rebellious force was in the form of a serpent god. In the mythology, the serpent god is eventually overthrown and cast into chaos.

Possibilities of where Rowling is going with this:

1) **Locations**. We already know that the second Fantastic Beasts movie will be based in Paris. As Pherecydes speaks of five recesses of the cosmos, could each movie have its base in one of these recesses? And would the recess be a location or an element?

2) **The Pentagram**—For Pherecydes, the five recesses and elements came together to form the image of the pentagram. It would be wonderful if, when all five main locations of the FB films are known, you could draw a pentagram between their location points.

In such a manner, it could be shown that the magic is spreading and coming together to form a protective magical amulet for the world. While this is a cool thought, it may not be logistically possible to make it happen in the cities of the world Rowling wishes to set the story. Therefore, the five recesses may take on a more symbolic representation through the elements they represent, which will be harder to pinpoint until the movies are viewed.

The fifth recess is the most intriguing. Pherecydes is credited as the first in western thought to develop the belief of the soul. He is also credited with defining the concept of *metempsychosis*. Metempsychosis is the belief in the transmigration of souls. But what's intriguing about it for this series is that the souls can migrate *from human to animal or from animal to human.*

The Obscurus is Beast. Credence is Human. Interesting possibilities emerge, which I'll discuss more below.

Finally, there was a winged oak image associated with Pherecydes, a living representation of the Tree of Life. Considering the living Golden Leaves seen within Newt's trunk, this image intrigues me greatly. For more, see the Beast chapter.

The beliefs of Pherecydes and his student Pythagoras are rich with possibilities for this series. I'll cover it in more detail as time and research permit on my blog. Please join me there.

Obscurus/Obscurial

Many elements of the relationship between the Obscurial, the human host, and the Obscurus, the parasite, appear to represent demonic possession. The Obscurus takes control of Credence, at least initially, without his control or his awareness. We see Credence searching for this child Graves has envisioned. As Credence "scrabbles" under Modesty's bed, looking for evidence, he believes her to be the one. He is unaware that it is he who is causing the destruction until the end.

I also see hints of paranormal kinetic energy, a type of psychokinesis. In fact, Rowling specifically uses *kinetic* twice when describing the energy of the Obscurus. According to the first law of thermodynamics, energy within a system cannot be created or destroyed. But it can be transformed. The basic idea behind paranormal kinetic energy is that a supernatural force draws upon the energy of its surrounding environment to power itself. Thus the Obscurus could be feeding off the emotion and energy of not only Credence, but the entire city of New York. A city seething underneath with this brewing battle between magical and No-Maj. Think how powerful the Obscurus could become amid the negative energy fueled by a world war.

However, the most intriguing link of possible origin for Rowling's creation is the one mentioned above: *metempsychosis*. Metempsychosis states that the mass of souls is finite and revolves in a cycle of endless reincarnation. When by death a soul is liberated from the prison of its human body, it may exist for a time in its free spirit form, but will eventually be bound again in another physical body. These cycles repeat endlessly from human to animal to human.

It's a theme that would tie interestingly to the nature of the Obscurus as both beast and human. Here we must consider another physics principle, the conservation of mass, that within a system, matter is never destroyed or created but may be rearranged. We have a perfect example of it in Rowling's verse with the Occamy's transition from solid to liquid as it shifts to fit into the space it inhabits.

Some other items to note when considering Rowling's creation of the Obscurus:

- The "publisher" for the 2001 *Fantastic Beasts* textbook was Obscurus books. Did she have this story in mind even then?
- Near the beginning, a No=Maj who saw the Obscurus mentions his "shinin white eyes" (p. 7). White is the color of death, and possibly a spell of mass killing.
- Newt met one in Sudan. Another hint toward a visit to Africa.
- I admit this one is a stretch, but through the International Confederation of Wizards' Swiss delegate, Eberstadt, Rowling hints at the German region that is home to Frankenstein's Castle. The full title of Mary Shelley's famous horror novel was *Frankenstein, or, The Modern Prometheus*. The myth of Prometheus giving fire to humans shows the what havoc is wrought when the power of the gods is released to humans.

Finally, I'd like to note the similarity of Credence to our former Potions Master. Snape. *Professor* Snape, that is. Like Snape, Credence is a child of an abusive home who longs for an important place in the wizarding world. He develops a fascination with a powerful, dark wizard who is keen to introduce him to the dark side of his powers.

However, at his core, Credence is a good soul, a hurt young man longing to be loved.

As such, like Snape, he is an antihero, a character of ambiguity, the hero of his own story, and a man most needing of redemption.

Serpent

Within the Slytherin section of the Theme chapter, I discuss how the Slytherin house and heritage gets a makeover as it travels across the Atlantic. The same is true of its mascot, the snake.

References to serpents or snakes within the text:

- The Horned Serpent who was useful to Isolt and represented the Horned Serpent House at Ilvermorny.
- The Snakewood tree that grows from Slytherin's wand, which

Isolt had buried on the grounds of Ilvermorny. Out of it grows a tree with leaves used in medicinal healing.

- The Occamy is a snake-like bird, and an adorable one at that.
- The belt that was whipped out of Mary Lou's hand when she tries to beat Credence is likened to a snake in its movements.
- The Runespoor on the cover of *Fantastic Beasts* is a three-headed serpent.

All are positive representations of snakes as even the belt is slithering away from Mary Lou's abusive intent.

Beyond these overt images of serpents are those I've mentioned as possible clues in the subtext. With a story where the hero is a Magizoologist and loves all his creatures, it's not surprising that the snake is represented in a more positive light.

River of Lethe

In ancient Greece, the river Lethe was one of the five rivers of the Underworld. As the dead passed through or drank its waters, their memories were erased. This cleansing was the only way they could pass on to the afterlife in the Elysium fields. Virgil further clarified that the dead must erase all memories of the former life to be reincarnated.

MACUSA must have imported some bottled water from the river Lethe, because the waters of "rippling potion" in their death chamber acts like a memory siphon and giant Pensieve to lull those about to be executed to death.

The executioner extracts Tina's happy memories to taunt her onto the death chair floating above the waters. She gazes down upon:

1) Her mother calling her pumpkin, calling her to bed
2) Tina in Second Salem Church, stopping Mary Lou's abuse with a spell and comforting Credence.

At this point, Pickett releases Newt. In his struggle to overpower the executioner, her wand drops into the pool. The waters transform into "vicious black bubbles" (p. 170), and Tina's memories turn dark.

3) Mary Lou threatens Tina and calls her a witch

As we are shown by what happens when the wand falls into the pool, the intended are executed by the rising flames-like waves of the black waters of death. Their final memories their worst.

Death by a brutal form of baptism.

Pentecost

While Rowling alluded to Jesus' sacrifice and resurrection in Harry Potter, I feel she may be heading toward Pentecost in Fantastic Beasts. Pentecost, meaning fifty days (there's that five theme again), is celebrated fifty days after the resurrections of Christ. In Acts 2, the disciples were gathered together and the Holy Spirit came down upon them like a "rushing, mighty wind." Flames appeared upon each person gathered, and they began to speak and understand each other's language. Even languages they had not known before. About three thousand were baptized that day.

The church credits Pentecost as the beginning of the church and celebrates it every year. It's a time of reaffirming the union of the church and the commitment to carry its message of healing and love throughout the world.

Why I think this links to Fantastic Beasts—the early church was very apocalyptic, believing Jesus' second coming would happen within their lifetime. They understood Pentecost as the day when God united them and gave them the tools to prepare for this event. It was their day of commission, their launch to go out and bring in new believers by spreading the good news that would save them all from future destruction.

If you read my section on the Holocaust and Atomic bomb, you'll understand where I believe Rowling to be headed for the end of this series. We've already seen the massive destruction one Obscurus wrought. If Grindelwald assembles a whole army of magical creatures with immense power, we will truly face an apocalyptic scenario.

I believe Newt and Team will be forced to combat this destruction and will unite an international league charged with forever after ensuring the survival of not only both No-Maj and Wizard, but fantastic magical beasts as well.

Looking Forward

As we saw repeatedly through Harry Potter, the myths and analogies that are most important, like alchemy, Rowling will draw from again and again. With these myths in mind, we'll be better prepared to analyze movie two when the previews start leaking!

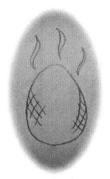

Secret Seven

Which Ships are Going to Sail?
(Romantic Relationships)

Newt literally sails into this new movie on a ship and leaves on one as well. Rowling's canon already tells us how his relationship with Tina will end. But what about the others? And what difficulties might Rowling throw at her star characters to slow down their happy ending?

For the double romance structure, I believe she is taking a lead from Jane Austen's *Pride and Prejudice*. Mr. Bingley, the bank manager, gives us a nod in this direction as he passes the baton, if not the money, to Jacob, his counterpart as the secondary hero and romantic figure.

Why *Pride and Prejudice*? First, because Rowling is an acknowledged Jane Austen fan.[15] She named Filch's cat Mrs. Norris after a disliked character in *Mansfield Park*.

More importantly, because she's playing off the romance of a couple facing an initial impression of distrust against a couple so delightfully positive and charming. Where Rowling will deviate from the Austenesque plan will surely provide some wonderful surprises along the way.

I'll be on the hunt for more hints of *Pride and Prejudice* as we go forward and hope you will join me!

Secrets of Relationships Explored:
1) Newt and Tina
2) Queenie and Jacob

---

[15] http://harrypotter.wikia.com/wiki/Jane_Austen

3) Graves and Credence
4) Newt and Leta
5) Queenie and Abernathy

Newt and Tina:

Where Tina and Newt come together is in their care and concern for children and beasts. Newt has charged himself with collecting and protecting magical creatures that the wizarding world would like to exterminate. The same is true for Tina in regard to children and the abused. She sacrificed her job to protect Credence. Together, Newt and Tina fight to protect those society has ignored, harmed, or is trying to drive into extinction.

We know they will end up together, but we don't know how much trouble and turmoil they will go through to earn their happily ever after. With Rowling, I imagine it will be a lot.

Queenie and Jacob

Queenie and Jacob are an adorable couple built on the attraction between a beautiful, free-spirited woman who seems eternally positive and an earnest and sincere man whose goal is to live while making others happy.

To me, Queenie and Jacob represent what could have been if Neville and Luna had gotten together, which was a match I shipped. Queenie has the same free-spirited attitude of Luna, even if Queenie is firmly focused on reality. She has to be. She can read others' minds.

In Jacob, I see a hint of Neville. Neville was always a bit of an outsider due to his lack of magical power early on. Jacob the No-Maj has no magical powers. Rowling, however, said in an interview that Jacob is like Ron, especially regarding his loyalty.

Unlike Newt and Tina, we cannot be sure this ship will sail through the end of the series. We do not know whether Queenie or Jacob will live or die or whether someone will end up coming between them. As such, I expect we will experience a painful separation on the good ship Jakweenie at some point.

However, Sleeping Beauty gives me hope. As Queenie's kiss protected the memories within Jacob's Sleeping Beauty, I believe we'll see this couple live to see their happily ever after. She is, after all, Queen Charming.

Grindelwald and Credence

Most Potter fans are very familiar with Rowling's 2007 statement at

Carnegie Hall that she always thought of Dumbledore as gay. He was involved with Grindelwald in his youth, which is partly why he got carried away with Grindelwald's anti-Muggle plans.

Since then, Rowling has further elaborated on this relationship. She said that while Dumbledore was infatuated with Grindelwald, Grindelwald desired more to use his friend's feelings for his own benefit.[16]

We see this same type of manipulation between Graves and Credence. There is a longing in Credence when he looks at Graves. The younger man craves the emotional attention Grindelwald provides to the point of being infatuated. In the scene where Graves gives Credence the Deathly Hallows symbol, he treats him like a lover.

> **Graves gently, almost seductively, moves his thumb across the cuts, healing them instantly. Credence stares.**
> **(p. 181)**

However, Rowling makes it clear that Grindelwald is simply manipulating these feelings to get what he wants from Credence. Credence realizes this himself, in the scene after the Obscurus has attacked and killed Mary Lou when Grindelwald calls him a Squib and tells him he's unteachable. That is the painful trigger which sets off the final storm of the Obscurus.

The agony of a lover's betrayal, of the realization that he'd been used, is the all-too human element of this magical tragedy. And this part of the story has not ended. It will only get worse. Grindelwald will escape from prison. Credence has survived. If the magic Credence possessed unaware caused the level of destruction we saw in New York, think what he can do now that he knows his powers and is seeking revenge.

Newt and Leta

We know very little at this point of their former relationship. According to Queenie's mindreading, it left Newt with a lot of pain (for more, see the Leta section in the Character chapter). Rowling revealed in a brief interview at the *Fantastic Beasts* premiere in London, the reason Newt was expelled was because he was covering for someone else. Surely Leta.

We know Leta will appear in future movies. Will their meeting be

---

16   http://www.snitchseeker.com/harry-potter-news/j-k-rowling-explains-grindelwald-and-dumbledores-relationship-dracos-wand-transfer-71142/

explosive? While we know by canon that Newt and Tina marry, I'm sure they will climb a rocky road before arriving at their happily ever after.

Queenie and Abernathy

While it's obvious that Abernathy has a thing for Queenie, it doesn't seem that his affections are returned. Should Abernathy appear in future movies, could he act in such a way as to cause trouble with her brewing relationship with Jacob?

This Jakweenie fan hopes not!

Looking Forward

On a final note, Rowling has stated that Dumbledore will play a significant role in the series and that he is at the age of his life where he is still exploring his sexuality. [17] We all know that his relationship with Grindelwald has come to an end. So, might we see Dumbledore in a relationship with another man? And if so, could it be someone we've already met?

---

[17]   http://variety.com/2016/film/news/fantastic-beasts-dumbledore-gay-jk-rowling-harry-potter-1201915037/

Secret Eight

A Niffler's Treasure

(Easter Eggs!)

Rowling loves to play with her reader and that includes hiding Easter Eggs through both the visuals of the film and the text of the script. Here are a few below that I found and loved. Hope you enjoy!

Quidditch Position

When Mary Lou Barebone asks Newt near the beginning of the film if he is a seeker after truth, he replies:

"I'm more of a chaser, really" (p. 13).

I love this exchange, not only for its hint at his position on the Quidditch pitch, but for more personal reasons. It was when I first read in *Sorcerer's Stone* of Harry earning the position of Seeker for the Gryffindor Quidditch team that the story deeply clicked with me. I knew instantly how Rowling was using the term Seeker because I'd always considered myself a seeker after truth...not that I'm alone in this. Here Rowling openly uses the whole phrase, even if from the mouth of a twisted woman.

Red and Yellow Flames

This one is very curious to me: The banner for The Second Salem Philanthropic Society shows hands breaking a wand in two amid flames that are red and yellow.

Red and yellow? What does that color combination remind you of? Gryffindor. While this could be coincidence, as flames are often described in this way, coincidence rarely happens around JK Rowling.

This use of Gryffindor's colors could be merely an Easter Egg reminding us of Harry's house, but I'm also wondering if we may see a darker side to Gryffindor in this series as we're also seeing a better side of Slytherin. In Mary Lou's ancient magical heritage, maybe she is descended from the home of the brave.

Ron and Hermione's Meeting

Newt—(pointing at hot dog mustard still on Tina's lips)
(p. 31).

Remember the smudge of dirt Hermione pointed out on Ron's nose when first meeting him onboard the Hogwarts Express? We know these new two are going to get on famously.

Mrs. Weasley's Clock

I'm sure many Potter fans thought, just like I did, when seeing the MACUSA threat-level clock—Mrs. Weasley! This new (old) clock that points to the danger of the American wizarding community's exposure to the No-Maj world looks remarkably similar in form and function to the one Mrs. Weasley used to track the safety of her family members. For more on the MACUSA clock, see the Plot chapter.

Ukrainian Ironbelly

The dragons Newt worked with on the Eastern Front remind us of a special scene in *Deathly Hallows*. When Harry, Hermione, and Ron escape from Gringotts, they do so on the back of the Ukrainian Ironbelly they rescued from his chains of servitude.

A Dozen Delightful Eggs

Here are a few other snippets that remind us of our Hogwarts home:

1) **Dumbledore making the news**—In the montage of newspapers that flash on the screen at the beginning of the film, Dumbledore grabs front page news a couple of times, once in *Transfiguration Today* for his article on Animagus, and one in *The Daily Prophet* for commenting on his article.
2) **Newt's scarf**—Newt's wearing his Hufflepuff House colors with pride.
3) Enchanted ceiling in MACUSA—Like the one at Hogwarts
4) **Paper mice**—In MACUSA, the enchanted paper mice that are memos remind us of the paper planes from the Ministry of Magic.

5) **Murtlap that attacks Jacob**—When Umbridge makes Harry write sentences carved into his own hand, Hermione treats him with Murtlap Essence.

6) **Merlin's beard**—A favorite oath from Potter days that Newt uses.

7) **Grindylows**—The water demons who attacked Harry in the Triwizard tournament seem to have kin living in Newt's case.

8) **Erumpent exploding the tree**—The horn that explodes in the Lovegood's home in *Deathly Hallows*.

9) **Debutante poster at The Blind Pig**—Reminiscent of the Fat Lady hiding the entrance to Gryffindor.

10) **Credence's hand wounds**—Provide an unhappy flashback to Harry's wounds from Umbridge's lines.

11) **Protective charm cast over the City Hall subway**—Like the one cast over Hogwarts before Voldemort's battle.

12) **JK Rowl**—Name of a pastry seen in Jacob's store at the end.

I'm sure there are many that I missed. Let me know in the BeastChaser.com blog the ones you find!

Secret Nine

Peering into the Probable Future

(Series Forecast)

Throughout this clue book, we've speculated a lot toward the next four movies. In this section, we'll bring it all together as to what we expect to see.

As films, I expect we'll continue with fast-paced, high energy films that take place over a few days.

Magical elements we expect to see in the upcoming series include the Gordian Knot, the pentagram, and the Elder Wand.

But let's get into some nitty, gritty specifics.

Five Films and Location

For Fantastic Beasts, five is the new seven.

Harry Potter's seven book framework was important to Rowling for many reasons, most of which point to alchemy. She has announced that Fantastic Beasts will span five movies, and it seems accepted that each will be in five principle locations. I feel confident in stating that five was not chosen for a flimsy reason. The most significant probably relates to an underlying theme.

I've got two guess alternatives toward the possible locations. **First: five movies, five continents** (combining Europe and Asia and excluding uninhabited Antarctica). This would be quite fitting if the series is a lead-in to WWII where the magical world unites in a show of unity…or breaks apart in chaos.

To frame each film, as she did with the Hogwarts Express, Newt will enter the city at the beginning and leaves at the end. His mode of transport may not always be by ship, however…if she wishes to incorporate the air, earth, water, fire them the ship may have hinted at for this first.

With Newt's bio detailing that he had traveled to 100 countries in search of magical creatures, it's fair to speculate that the five-film franchise will be set against an international backdrop, whether the cities span five continents or not.

Second guess—in the Pentagram Office scene, there are five wizarding world leaders who have speaking roles. One of them is Madam Picquery, who has been the government leader in this first movie. What if Rowling plans one of each of these per remaining film?

We already know that the next movie will be set primarily in Paris, though Rowling has said not exclusively. Where might future movies lead? My guesses:

1. Paris—with pop on over to the UK to visit old unnamed British envoy as well
2. Africa—Momolu Wotorson
3. Switzerland or Germany—Heinrich Eberstadt
4. Asia—Madam Ya Zhou

Africa has had numerous mentions throughout the film and its subtext. Also, maybe when we're in the UK, we can look up some of our favorite Potter ancestors as well.

Paris next

It's very hard to forecast when and why the next movie will be set in Paris. One reason for this is because we do not know how overt Rowling will make the prelude leading up to WWII. Will she keep the movies focused firmly in the wizarding world? Or start hinting more at what's brewing among the No-Maj? However, there is one event which intrigues me as a possibility.

On August 27, 1928, major world leaders met in Paris to sign the Kellogg-Briand Pact. At first signed by the US, France, and Germany, most other countries later joined in. Designed to eliminate war, the treaty had little effect except to provide a basis for punishing war crimes.

This pact would serve as a good reason to bring a team from MACUSA to Paris. Jacob could be present to either attend a pastry school or expand his business. And Newt…well, Newt could always be on the trail of a magical beast, such as the Nogtail or a Bundimun.

Five Schools

Rowling is fully aware of the spread of her fandom across the globe and eager to include *all* her fans in her magical world. She spent time prior to the release of *Fantastic Beasts* to provide background information on Pottermore regarding wizarding schools internationally. Although she mentions eleven established schools, information has been given only on eight thus far:

1) **Hogwarts**, location: Scotland
2) **Durmstrang**, location: far northern Europe
3) **Beauxbatons**, location: France Pyrenees (hmm…has a famous pastry maker former student)
4) **Ilvermorny** (see section in Worldbuilding chapter for more)
5) **Uagadou**, location: Africa, Mountains of the Moon
6) **Mahoutokoro**, location: Japan Minami Iwo Jima, (another island in this chain associated with WWII)
7) **Castelobruxo**, location: Brazil, in rainforest (advanced in Magizoology…interesting)
8) **Koldovstoretz**, location: Russia, (mentioned in *Wonderbook: Book of Potions*, Pottermore).

Though the schools themselves may not play a significant role in the *Fantastic Beasts* series as we're dealing with a more adult cast, I imagine we'll encounter witches and wizards trained at each one of these as we travel from country to country, film to film.

Five Cultures

Rowling seems intent with this new series to set her cast against a wider ethnic backdrop. However, with the backlash she faced from using the living beliefs of Native Americans, she has already stumbled in venturing outside her native turf.

Keeping tight-lipped secrets regarding what was to come in Harry Potter was a huge part of what led to the books' success. But she's making movies now with a much larger crew involved.

Will we see her make a more concerted effort to partner with any marginalized voices she may draw into her world, especially concerning their mythology or living beliefs?

Indiana Jones in the Wizarding World?

Why was Grindelwald in New York City in the first place? Did he just happen to chance upon an Obscurus as he traveled the world raising followers? Or was Credence the sole reason for his visit?

My guess is that Grindelwald is doing what we have so often heard the Nazis did before and during World War II: seeking out supernatural relics or elements to aid him in his quest. We already know that Grindelwald sought to unite the Deathly Hallows. In the first film, he wanted to "use" the Obscurial for the Greater Good.

Each book may present a different magical power...or beast...that Grindelwald seeks to exploit. Let's just hope Indiana Newt...and Team...are up to the challenge of stopping him.

Missing Magical Elements

We did not clearly see an Animagi in the first movie, nor a Metamorphagus. I've discussed my theory regarding a hidden Animagi in the Plot chapter earlier. Whether it is Tina, as I expect, or Newt, I fully believe we will see one...of each of them.

Rowling is also taking advantage of the new series to introduce some new magical elements into her world, with the Obscurus being the primary example. What other treats might she have in store for her faithful fans?

I'm most suspicious of Grindelwald's visions and doubt seriously that they are a traditional Seer's. Perhaps we will see more clues as to what he's capable of in the next movie.

Secondary Characters to Watch For

With the understanding that the forthcoming films will be set in various countries, I do not expect most the secondary characters of this first movie to continue. Undoubtedly, however, some of them will.

Aside from the Team, Grindelwald, and Credence, my best bets lie with Modesty Barebone, Langdon Shaw, the named wizards in the International Confederation of Wizards meeting (for full discussion see that section in the Worldbuilding chapter), and of course Leta Lestrange.

Modesty is one of the few whom I think can reach Credence and help turn him around. With the Shaws, we must not forget the photos of the Obscurus, which may have survived Frank's obliviating shower. Langdon, in his fascination with magic and his desire to prove himself to his father, would be the key person to bring those photos to light. And Leta...well she's going to be the thorn in Newt and Tina's blossoming romance.

The International wizards will doubtlessly play a large role in the film set in their territory. Finally, we may see some of the minor characters pop up overseas as they go off to war. Doubtless, there will be casualties.

Modesty and Credence

I believe we will see Modesty play a powerful role in the series going forward. Based on my analysis in the Character section on her name among the Barebone children, I think she may play a pivotal role in saving Credence. For I absolutely believe he will be find peace by series' end.

Villain in Disguise

Rowling continues with her favored villain in disguise technique from the Harry Potter stories. Therefore, we must be on the alert throughout the next movie, and what hints we may receive in the release of information and trailers prior to it. *Constant vigilance*! Or, as MACUSA puts it on their eye-triangle logo: **Always Stay Vigilant!**

As Rowling used a new villain and a new twist with each book in Harry Potter, I would expect her to continue likewise throughout *Fantastic Beasts*. Also, I would not be a bit surprised to find a returning character, perhaps a minor one like Abernathy, suddenly twisted into a supporter of Grindelwald's. Many Aurors heard him speak in the subway. Surely some of them thought he had the right of it.

Who is to Die

As the Harry Potter series was releasing, one of the central questions for speculation among fans became who was to die in the next book. For *Fantastic Beasts*, with a world war looming, I'm afraid there will be many deaths before the end.

Perhaps the greatest question would be regarding the central team. Fortunately, unless Rowling chooses to go against her already established canon, we know that Newt and Tina will both survive and marry. Unfortunately, the same cannot be said for Queenie and Jacob. As a fan of their characters and a Jakweenie shipper, I really hope they will survive. But, as dark as I expect Rowling is going, I doubt they both will. The tea leaves are too murky this early in the series to make a serious prediction, but my hunch is that as No-Maj Jacob would be the most likely to die, it will instead be Queenie. I could see her sacrificing herself to save her love.

For the others, we know according to canon that Grindelwald survives…at least until he meets Voldemort. While I hope Credence can be saved and live to see a peaceful life where he comes into his own as a wizard, I'm afraid that he may achieve peace shortly before dying.

I could see Madam Picquery being assassinated, or any one of the named wizards in the International Confederation of Wizards scene.

As long as no beasts die in the making of these movies, all will be good. But, with the possibility of a beast used as a weapon of mass destruction, I worry about the safety of Frank and Swooping Evil.

Holocaust and Atomic Bomb

I did not start out this study looking for an atomic bomb. The theory came by way of the evidence presented through the film and script book. There are just too many allusions to a weapon of mass destruction to be cast aside. And we know the mass killings that occurred throughout WWII until the end.

Whether Rowling will venture so far into the No-Maj world as to make the historical Holocaust and atomic bombing of Hiroshima and Nagasaki a part of the series, I do not know. But I'm sure there will be at least a magical counterpart to it.

Starting with the white light killing spell that Grindelwald used in the beginning to kill five Aurors at once, weapons of mass destruction have played an important role in this story. As the Obscurus implodes at the end, the language used is very evocative of fallout from a fission explosion.

Then we must consider where the story takes place. New York City. The Manhattan Project that developed the US's atomic bomb was named because the Army Corp of Engineers division that started the project, though it later progressed to other areas throughout the country, was based in Manhattan.

Newt

Mass slaughter for the greater good, you mean? (p. 158)

With these words, Newt sharpens the focus to both the Holocaust and the Atomic bomb. From this pivotal scene where he is interrogated by Graves, to the end revelation of Grindelwald, the Obscurial, and Grindelwald's desire to exploit him, carries the momentum of the story.

Consider too the sharp division between wizard and No-Maj presented through the film. The divide and distrust, where "when No-Majs are afraid, they attack" (p. 42) is a setup for a mass killing along ethnic lines.

Other bits of evidence pointing to a Holocaust or Atomic bomb scenario:

- The name of the Swiss delegate in the Pentagram Office hints at a link to Heinrich Himmler, the mastermind of the concentration camps.
- Rowling has carefully included characters of Jewish origin—

the Goldstein sisters, and possibly Jacob.

- The Queen Esther reference from both Queenie and Tina's middle name hints at a mass slaughter of Jewish people.
- The Thunderbird ending with a venomous potion released onto a whole city is probably a prelude for worse things to come.

Dark days lie ahead. Fortunately, Rowling never leaves her reader or characters without the love of friends and family to see them through.

Questions Remaining

Here are a few niggling questions I'm left to ponder:

Newt's Case

Graves had control of Newt's case from the time Newt and Tina were thrown in jail until Queenie stole it out of his office the next day. Knowing that Grindelwald seems to be as fascinated as Newt with the power of the beasts, but for different purposes, would he not have taken the opportunity to examine that case thoroughly? Considering that he had overnight to explore Newt's secret world and creatures, I expect to see a mystery thread regarding what Grindelwald did in there in the next movie. Keep in mind, however, that Grindelwald never believed he would lose control of the case.

Also, Newt *may* have given his old case to Jacob at the end—that catch flicking open is certainly suspicious (see p. 271). Will this cause another mixup in the next movie? If Newt has transferred all his beasts to a new case, one he now ties up with string to ensure its security, would anything Grindelwald left behind be in Newt's case…or Jacob's?

Photos

Shaw's reporter took photos of the subway during the Obscurus attack. Did the magical rain erase these images, or will they resurface? Langdon could surely use them to his advantage with his father.

Jacob's Memories

As Jacob stood under the obliviating rain, Queenie shielded him with an umbrella and kissed him. From the beastly shapes of some of his pastries once he opened his shop, it seems a hint of memory lingers on. Then, finally, when Queenie walks into his shop, he smiles.

Perhaps he has not forgotten everything after all. And perhaps true love's first kiss shielded this sleeping beauty until his Queen Charming could return.

Will *all* Jacob's memories return?

Swooping Evil

Continuing with the question of memories, could the Swooping Evil potion at the end of the film be a prelude for things to come? Could something so magically atrocious occur that the whole world's memory must be erased?

Deathly Hallows Symbol

Graves/Grindelwald gives Credence a Deathly Hallows symbol which can be used to summon him. As we know Credence still lives, and he probably still has that symbol, how will he use it?

Newt's Role as a Scientist

What if Newt, in his desire to conserve the beasts, is unwittingly the scientist who provides Grindelwald with the weapon of mass destruction? Is the power Newt unleashed with Swooping Evil a foretaste of what's to come? **Could this meek, shy, awkward, and gentle man create a weapon capable of such destruction? Or will his role come in putting a stop to the one the Muggles are creating?**

Finally, I'm going to go out on a Whomping Willow limb here and suggest that near series end we're going to see Newt reunited with Frank. What I can imagine is a post-war scene where Newt and Tina travel to Arizona for some healing time and are reunited with the Thunderbird in an emotional reunion. Or perhaps Frank would come to Newt's aid in a highly climatic scene, and then carry him "home" to heal.

It's Rowling's imagination that matters, but I do believe we will see the two reunited.

Where to Go From Here

I've enjoyed sharing these theories with you, and I will enjoy even more hearing yours. Please join me on my BeastChaser.com blog to continue the speculation. As time permits, I'll cover more topics and deepen those already started. I'd love to share your theories with other fans as well.

Then we'll all be fully prepared when the new clues start Rowling in for Fantastic Beasts 2!

For other great fansites that cover Rowling's Wizarding World, be sure to check out:

- Pottermore.com
- AlwaysJKRowling.com
- Mugglenet.com
- The-Leaky-Cauldron.org
- SnitchSeeker.com
- Hypable.com
- HP-Lexicon.org
- HarryPotter.wikia.com
- HarryPotterForWriter.com
- BeastChaser.com

Finally, if you enjoyed the material in this clue book, please consider leaving a review at your favorite online site.

As we have four exciting movies to come, I will not say goodbye. Instead, let's say—

Nox!

List of Publications

Soon To Be Released:

Call of the Jinn, a young adult fantasy

Previously Published:

- *Teaching Harry Potter to Creative Writers: An Educator's Guide*—November 2016
- *A Writer's Guide to Harry Potter*—July 2016
- *Southern Fried Wiccan*—March 2015
- "Lighting the Sacred Way" in *Journeys of Wonder 2*—October 2012
- "Running Raw" in *Sweeter Than Tea*—June 2012
- *Egyptian Myths in Harry Potter*, an editorial in three parts; Mugglenet.com—July 2007
- "Grandma's Cupboards" in *On Grandma's Porch*—June 2007
- *One Last Memory*; a Featured Editorial on Mugglenet—Feb. 2007
- "From Online to Paperback: The Making of The Plot Thickens" and "Geomancy and Alchemy in Harry Potter" in *Proceedings of Accio UK 2005*—July 2006
- *Ultimate Unofficial Guide to the Mysteries of Harry Potter: Analysis of Book 5*; by Galadriel Waters; Wizarding World Press—June 2005. (editor and contributor.)
- "A Family Treasure" in *More Sweet Tea*—April 2005
- "Chamber of Thoth" and "Geomancy and Alchemy Gems in Harry Potter" in *The Plot Thickens...Harry Potter Investigated by Fans for Fans*; Wizarding World Press—November 2004

Please check out my blog at HarryPotterforWriters.com and Twitter feed @HP4Writers for continued discussion of how we can improve our writing with Harry Potter as our text.

About the Author

S.P. Sipal is a writer, editor, and international speaker who has unearthed the secrets Rowling hides within her text since the Harry Potter phenomenon gripped the nation. Susan celebrated the release of the last Harry Potter book, *Deathly Hallows*, as a presenter at a fan conference in London. Her writing workshops, school and college lessons, and numerous fan conference presentations have been met with enthusiasm and repeat requests.

Susan lives in North Carolina with her husband and two children. You can find her on Twitter @HP4Writers, her website at SPSipal.com, and her blog at BeastChaser.com and HarryPotterforWriters.com.

If you liked the material in this guide, please consider leaving a review at your favorite review site.

To book Susan for speaking engagements, interviews, and other Harry Potter or writing events, please contact publicity@DeepRiverPressInc.com.

Acknowledgements

Thank you to everyone who worked as a team, on a *very* short amount of time, to make this clue book possible:

- To Greg Schultz for the breathtaking cover. You truly outdid yourself this time!
- To Kayla Laine Perkinson for beautifully drawn and fan-inspired illustrations that liven up all these words.
- To Dalton Perkinson and Lora Sipal for their support and patience that helped keep me sane and able to work.
- To Altug, for putting up with me being gone, even when I was there.
- To Lisa London for making it happen…once again.
- To Annie Battista, for her wonderful observations.
- Most of all, to JK Rowling for revealing a fresh new corner of her inspiring world for us to play in.

Index

Made in the USA
Lexington, KY
18 January 2018